THE IMAGE MAKER

STUDY GUIDE

TERRY M. CRIST

It is said that the number one problem of twenty-first-century man is an identity crisis. From my many years of counseling and training thousands in self-development, I would agree that this crisis is critical. *The Image Maker* is a masterpiece toward helping us solve this challenge. Terry Crist has made his mark with this exceptional work. Everyone should read this one.

—DR. MYLES MUNROE, SENIOR PASTOR
BAHAMAS FAITH MINISTRIES INTERNATIONAL
FOUNDER OF THE DIPLOMAT CENTER

With the skill of a wordsmith and the research of a teacher, Terry Crist uncovers truth regarding our being "made in the image of God." He chips away at what doesn't belong and, like a master sculptor, leaves only what is needed. The result of reading this book should be a restoration of self-worth without pride.

—TOMMY TENNEY, FOUNDER OF THE GODCHASERS NETWORK
AUTHOR OF *THE GOD CHASERS* AND *GOD'S DREAM TEAM*

The Image Maker may well be one of the most important books of this generation. In a world that knows that the lack of self-esteem means ultimate failure, we look in vain for an image of ourselves that will give our lives fulfillment, purpose, meaning and success. Never before have I read a manuscript that describes the radical nature of the new birth as does this one. It is this experience that gives us our true self-worth based upon who we are in Christ—not a self-esteem based upon your performance. *The Image Maker* is the book that had to be written and the book that must be read!

—TOMMY REID, SENIOR PASTOR
THE TABERNACLE, BUFFALO, NY

Your vision for *The Image Maker*, to awaken believers to the beauty of union with Christ and the security that comes in identifying with Him, was academically, professionally, scripturally and spiritually accomplished. I finished the manuscript wanting more! Your book brings the power of Christ's atoning work for all who dare to believe. I believe every "born of the Spirit" person should be given a copy of this book to read to help them continue to walk in their union with Christ.

—DR. DIANNE MCINTOSH, PH.D.
THE GRACE MINISTRY

Terry Crist brilliantly navigates us through the turbulent waters of the self-esteem movement. With biblical insight and heartfelt inspiration, we discover the wonder of God and the magnificent worth of those who bear His image. This is a life-changing book.

—TOM MOFFETT, SENIOR PASTOR
EVANGELISTIC TEMPLE, HOUSTON, TX

Be free to accept that you are fearfully and wonderfully made. In Terry Crist's new book, *The Image Maker*, you will discover that as a child of God you can be delivered from insignificance and insecurity. Written with a prophetic edge that speaks straight to your heart, this book will loose you to discover the true you. You can become who you really are.

—JOHN MASON
AUTHOR OF *AN ENEMY CALLED AVERAGE* AND
YOU'RE AN ORIGINAL, DON'T DIE A COPY

A deep and far-reaching study on personal image and destiny.

—COLIN DYE, SENIOR PASTOR
KENSINGTON TEMPLE, LONDON, ENGLAND

In this signature book, Terry Crist skillfully excavates the mysteries of the new creation to help you discover and cultivate a truly liberated life—a life free from the curse of a mistaken identity! The insights, wisdom and mature illustrations describe in detail God's master plan for an entire new humanity. Revelatory and challenging!

—MIKE BICKLE, FOUNDER
INTERNATIONAL HOUSE OF PRAYER
KANSAS CITY, MO

The Image Maker is a gourmet meal of spiritual and intelligent thought from the heart and soul of Terry Crist. There are books that bless and encourage, and there are books that can change a life. Read this book carefully. There is change between the pages!

—DICK BERNAL, FOUNDER/SENIOR PASTOR
JUBILEE CHRISTIAN CENTER
SAN JOSE, CA

"Terry was a wonderful guest on my radio show. His helpful and candid approach to who we are in Christ prompted my audience to respond. He really made them think! His fresh insight and profound examinations give new meaning to what Christ should be to all of us. *The Image Maker* is an important book that will affirm your faith."

—HOLLY MCCLURE, SYNDICATED MOVIE CRITIC
RADIO TALK SHOW HOST
KPRZ, CALIFORNIA

Xulon Press
11350 Random Hills Road
Suite 800
Fairfax, VA 22030
(703) 279-6511
XulonPress.com

CONTENTS

PART III: DETERMINING YOUR MISSION

FOREWORD

I have been privileged to nurture, feed and direct some of the
Lord's sheep and lambs under His direct supervision. Often in
my involvement in the "people-helping" business, I have had to
come alongside them in the power of the Holy Spirit and act as a
"midwife" in the birth process of their experience of their unique
and true worth in Christ. In recent years I have come to feel a great
deal of empathy with them in the light of my own struggles and
challenges as it relates to celebrating whom God has made us to be.
I have come to believe that as spiritual friends of the Bridegroom we
are to bring His loving and healing presence into their existence at
a deeper and more profound level. Often I find that their misbelief
and their limited belief is at the root of their emotional pain.
Helping them recognize their inadequate mental models and
encouraging them in the process of the renewing of their minds take
a great deal of time, patience and process.

My trusted friend Terry Crist has given us some of the tools that
invite us to reconsider the mental models we unconsciously
embrace that rob us of the truth that sets us free. It seems as though
he is inviting us to repent of far more than our inadequate performance in the area of pleasing God. His invitation is that we "dump
our files" of our inaccurate and inadequate beliefs about who we
think we are and embrace by faith whom God truly calls us to be
and become. There is a great deal to contemplate and consider in
this millennial apologetic on the "new man." Whether your personal
study on the new creation has ever led you this far or not, one thing
is for certain: The Image Maker will cause you to take a fresh look
at one of the great truths of your redemption in Christ and to cele-

brate your true value as a child of the Father.

One poignant moment in The Image Maker that gripped my heart is the story of Terry's personal encounter in the dentist office with an out-of-touch and incongruent father and his precious daughter suffering from Down's syndrome. I was reminded of our considerable need for agents of healing in society. May you find great encouragement and a rich resource of the Spirit of life in Christ Jesus as you peruse the pages of this thorough and well-done treatise.

—Dr. Mark Chironna
The Master's Touch International Church
Orlando, Florida

INTRODUCTION

T he search for self-esteem has rapidly become the Holy Grail of the twenty-first century. In the quest to discover our inherent worth, many Christians have become vulnerable to the ancient enemies of humanism and pantheism. This battle is not just being waged in the New Age community; it has invaded the church through a subtle distortion of the biblical principles of "identity, image and design."

Many contemporary self-help gurus suggest that the reason people are so defeated in life is simply because they "don't feel good about themselves." The apparent mission of the self-esteem "movement" is to deceive you into believing that self-esteem is essential for your psychological well-being. In this study guide, I address this issue directly, because there is a vast difference between the concept of **self-esteem** and the truth concerning our individual **self-worth**.

Let's begin by contrasting the principles of self-esteem with the biblical concept of self-worth. William James,[1] considered by many to be the father of American psychology, defined self-esteem this way:

$$\text{Self-esteem} = \underline{\text{Success / Pretensions}}$$

Based on that definition, self-esteem is a reflection of how you are performing (your successes) compared to how you think you should be performing (your pretensions). If you accept that definition, your self-esteem should fluctuate each day based upon your actions in life. This also may cause you to seek the approval of man at the expense of God's will for your life.

Self-worth, on the other hand, is an entirely different matter. Our value as human beings is not based upon any of our personal abilities. It is predicated upon one simple fact: The infinite Creator of the universe created us in His personal image. Because of that, man's basic worth never fluctuates because it is secure in the identity of The Image Maker—not the image bearer. So, while your self-esteem goes up and down, your essential worth and value are forever stable. Even though you may *feel* worthless at times and extremely worthwhile at other times, those feelings do not change the fact that The Image Maker considers you "fearfully and wonderfully" made. Self-esteem is based upon what you feel, but self-worth is based upon who you are.

Another way of contrasting these two opposing paradigms is to say that self-esteem is based upon performance, but self-worth is based upon an understanding of your identity. That understanding can be regained only through a personal relationship with The Image Maker.

The lessons in this study guide are designed to open your eyes to your essential worth and value, to help you discover your true identity, and to enable you to determine your personal destiny and purpose in life.

A NOTE TO STUDENTS AND GROUP LEADERS

We highly recommend that group leaders using this material in a classroom setting will have already read, or will read in conjunction with this study, the complete text of *The Image Maker* by Terry Crist. While these lessons will stand alone with the accompanying text, we encourage all students to broaden the scope of this study by reading the complete text of *The Image Maker.*

PART I:
DESIGNED AND DEFINED

LESSON ONE
HOW IN THE WORLD DID WE GET HERE?

We should have seen it coming. Warning signs abounded. In less than two generations, policy violations in school shifted from talking in class, chewing gum, and running in the halls to drug abuse, physical assault, robbery and murder. When the senseless slaughter at Littleton, Colorado shocked the nation, the question on the lips of almost everyone was "Why?" Cultural analysts dissected every imaginable motive, but found no answers. Rather than asking "Why?" perhaps the more accurate question was "Why not?"

Why not? What else can we expect from teenagers who have been told that ideas and actions are without consequences and that we are just occupying one empty moment on the evolutionary road to nowhere? A young songwriter summarized the hopelessness contained within the heart of this generation. "I belong to the Blank Generation. I have no beliefs. I belong to no community, tradition or anything like that. I'm lost in this vast, vast world. I belong nowhere. I have absolutely no identity."[1] No identity, no beliefs, and no traditions translates to no responsibility, no respect, and no regard for human life.

THE LONG ROAD TO NOWHERE

At the close of the nineteenth century, most people in Western culture believed that God existed, had created the world and had established a certain value system, which was reflected in the Bible. Even non-professing Christians basically agreed with the need for moral standards in society. But that common consent began to unravel, and it has been deteriorating substantially with every decade since.

Three philosophical theories invaded the value system of both Christians and non-Christians in Western culture during the twentieth century.

The theory of evolution. Charles Darwin and other scientists challenged the biblical model of creation. Scientists then began to declare that people were simply the product of chance and natural selection. For the first time in Western society, the identity of man was under question.

The purpose of our existence debate naturally followed the theory of evolution. Philosophers deduced that if we were not here because a loving God created us in His image, then personal destiny was a concept to be rejected. Men and women began to question their purpose in life, and this led to disillusionment and despair in our culture.

Throughout the ages, to know and fully understand the origin, purpose and destiny of man has been an ongoing quest. However, the question, "Who am I?" cannot be answered apart from a biblical understanding of the original image and ultimate purpose of man. When the question of "Who am I?" is answered with "You are nothing—just a blob that crawled out of the swamp, and when your time on earth is over, you'll still be nothing," then what can we expect but hopelessness, despair, and a "who cares what I do" attitude.

Moral absolutes were replaced by ethical relativism, further widening the philosophical gap. If the God of the Bible did not exist, then the moral standards of the Bible should be rejected as well. These issues have developed for decades, until by now most people are convinced that absolute truth (including moral truth) does not exist.

The invasion of Eastern mysticism in the 1960's enhanced Darwin's theory of evolution by making the Bible appear as just another religious alternative. Questions of purpose and existence caused many to turn to drugs and Eastern spiritualism. The concepts of reincarnation swept through a spiritually hungry populace, spawning hundreds of new cults. Contemporary society continued to devalue the worth of an individual human being, resulting in an identity crisis in the soul of this generation.

How in the World Did We Get Here?

SEARCHING FOR AN IDENTITY

I am convinced that this generation will never settle the mystery of God as long as we ignore the mystery of man. To paraphrase 1 John 4:20, "If you fail to identify your brother whom you have seen, how can you identify God whom you have not seen?" Blindness to the basic worth of mankind prevents us from even acknowledging the existence of God. To devalue the creation is to deny the Creator. To devalue the identity of the image bearer is to deny the creatorial right of The Image Maker.

When we refuse to acknowledge who we are as image bearers of the Omnipotent One, we deny our right to dominion and authority.

When we refuse to acknowledge who we are as image bearers of the Omniscient One, we deny our right to know the truth.

When we refuse to acknowledge who we are as image bearers of the Omnipresent One, we deny our right to live in his presence.

CREATION CONFIRMS THE EXISTENCE OF GOD

"Since the creation of the world His invisible attributes are clearly seen, being understood by the things that are made, even His eternal power and Godhead, so that they [mankind] are without excuse."

—*Romans 1:20*

I have been privileged to stand on the top of a rugged mountain peak and view uninhabited valleys below, to lie in a sleeping bag and stare up at the Northern Lights displaying the celestial wonders of the heavens, or watch the Southern Cross from the jungles of central Africa—all compelling evidence of the existence of God. But none of these natural wonders testify of sovereign deity any greater than the mystery of man. No wonder mankind has been under attack from the beginning.

The human frame is, in the words of the psalmist David, "fearfully and wonderfully made" (Psalm 139:14). As geneticists unlock more and more of the mysteries of the structure of the human body, they validate the psalmists's words. Their discoveries in the field of DNA leave us awestruck at the complexity of the human construction.

Playwright Tom Stoppard said, "The idea of God is slightly more plausible than the alternative proposition that, given enough time, some green slime could write Shakespeare's sonnets."[2]

Secular humanism has no logical basis without the theory of evolution. The humanistic aim is to rid society of the presence of the Creator by denying that man is created in God's image. No humanist has been heard any louder in this generation than Charles Darwin. He crusaded to eradicate the existence of God from the minds of men by scientifically challenging the concepts of design and purpose. His ideas later formed the basis of thought for John Dewey, who in turn had a profound influence on the development of our educational system.

EVOLUTION PRODUCES REVOLUTION

Violence has prevailed where Darwinism has ruled as the predominant worldview. The Franco-Prussian War of 1870 set the philosophical course for literally hundreds of subsequent conflicts by using Darwin's theory as the basis for militant oppression. In more recent times, China, Russia and Nazi Germany provide documentation for the abuse of human rights based upon their antitheistic worldview. Even the demonized drive toward "ethnic cleansing" in Eastern Europe has its roots in the soil of natural selection.

Karl Marx was proud to acknowledge Charles Darwin's theory as the scientific basis for his views on class struggle. Marxism was once defined as "Darwinism applied to human society."[3] Joseph Stalin boastfully declared that "evolution prepares for revolution and creates the ground for it. Revolution consummates the process of evolution and facilitates its further activity."[4]

EVOLUTION LAYS THE GROUNDWORK FOR SOCIAL SAVAGERY

When a man believes that he is nothing more than an evolved animal, he subconsciously settles for life at its lowest common denominator. (The natural instinct to survive and procreate is endemic to wild animals.) And when man believes that he is nothing more than the product of colliding dust particles, it is no wonder he struggles with a lack of worth and value. But when man believes that he is the product of divine design, created by The Image Maker, then that man will rise to discover his personal destiny in life.

Many people who give casual mental assent to the theory of evolution would be shocked at the social ramifications of Darwin's views on the purpose of man. His 1859 book, *The Origin of the Species*, was subtitled *The Preservation of Favored Races in the Struggle for Life.* Darwin openly taught that all whites would eventually kill all blacks—as well as the other "lower races" —within a century or two. This would merely be ongoing evolutionary development in progress. Adolph Hitler's most notorious work, *Mein Kampf (My Struggle)*, was based upon evolutionary theory. Hitler publicly aligned himself with Darwin, identifying him as a prophet with special insight into the history of man and the future of the species.

When the belief that God created the heavens and the earth is rejected (as many do in our day), basic human rights are reinterpreted and, in some cases, even exterminated. The Declaration of Independence bases its doctrine of "unalienable rights" upon the doctrine of creation: "Men are endowed by their Creator with certain unalienable rights, that among these are life, liberty and the pursuit of happiness."

To remove the presence of the Creator, you remove the basis for "unalienable rights." That's why racism is not just a sin against humanity, but it is ultimately a sin against The Image Maker. Racism spurns the creative handiwork of a sovereign God who created *all* men in His image and likeness. The very word *human* means "shaded or colored man." Black, brown, peach, white, red and yellow, we reflect another dimension of His divine image. But more importantly, more fundamentally, John 4:24 declares that God is Spirit. Regardless of color or shade, all men are created in the image of the Creator who is Spirit.

When we believe that we have been carefully constructed in the likeness and image of a personal being—even apart from the spiritual issues—the constitution of natural life has great value and sacred implications. Human life contains unmatched value in the created order of all life forms. What sets man, the image bearer, apart from the rest of creation is the **purpose** of his original design.

The New Age worldview maintains that all life has equal value. According to Ingrid Newkirk, president of People for the Ethical Treatment of Animals, "A rat is a pig is a dog is a boy."[5] I have often wondered what psychological effect this must have on the child who believes that his life is the equivalent of ham and eggs. Furthermore, what must register in the heart of this generation when many of the same people protesting to save the whales also protect the right to murder unborn babies?

We are sending mixed signals to this generation. The principles of evolution and special creation are philosophically opposed to one another. They will not coexist. Ravi Zacharias, the brilliant Christian apologist, recently wrote, "We have given our children contradictory assumptions about life and then are shocked at their evil behavior and the disintegration of their lives."[6]

Ironically, in a politically correct, religiously tolerant, multicultural society, we still subtly reinforce the principles of male chauvinism, class segregation and racial oppression because of the underpinnings of evolution in our educational system. While paying lip service to the principles of tolerance and diversity, our public schools continue to teach the amoral values of natural selection. In textbooks, motion pictures, and video games, evolutionary theory continues to shape the collective conscience of our nation.

While recently ministering to a young man struggling with his purpose in life, I heard the Holy Spirit speak words that shocked my mind and broke my heart. He said, "This young man cannot see his purpose because he has never embraced his worth."

We cannot systematically debase a generation through distorted instructions and still expect them to have a healthy view of the worth of man. What we devalue in the classroom we destroy in the streets. As we dispose of our unwanted fetuses, we bury our young in increasing numbers. The cries of pain in the abortion clinics are muffled by the sounds of gunfire in our streets. To the calloused humanist, this may simply be the modern urban equivalent of the "survival of the fittest."

On the fateful morning following the Columbine High School massacre, I read the bold headlines screaming from the paper, "Our Kids Are Crying Bullets." Tears ran down my cheeks and I thought of the words of the song, "Hands" by Jewel Kilcher, "If I could tell the world just one thing, it would be that we're all OK...."[7] Sorry, Jewel, we're not OK.

DISCOVERING YOUR IMAGE

Several principles incorporated in this lesson are listed below. In your own words, write a brief summary of each principle as you understand it. Or, if you choose, you may copy one or two statements from the lesson.

1. During the twentieth century three philosophical theories invaded the value system of Western culture, affecting Christians and non-Christians alike.

2. This generation will never settle the mystery of God as long as we ignore the mystery of man.

3. Creation confirms the existence of God.

4. Evolution lays the groundwork for social savagery.

5. What sets man—the image bearer—apart from the rest of creation is the purpose of his original design.

6. The principles of evolution and special creation are philosophically opposed to one another. They will not coexist.

FORMING YOUR IMAGE

The following principles are presented in a format that focuses on personal application. In the space provided after each, write what seems applicable to you.

1. I am aware that the theory of evolution has affected me in the following ways .

2. To me, the phrase "mystery of man" means . . . .

3. I see creation confirming the existence of God in the following areas. . . .

4. I recognize that the theory of evolution excuses social savagery in the following ways. Be specific.

5. Have I embraced the purpose of God's original design for my life? Yes___ No___ Explain

6. If you recognize that in some areas you have tried to embrace both the principles of evolution and special creation, what adjustments in your beliefs are needed?

REINFORCING YOUR IMAGE—PERSONAL REVIEW

True/False

1. At the close of the nineteenth century, most people in Western culture believed that God existed and had created the world. True_____ False_____

2. It is possible to understand the mystery of God without understanding the mystery of man. True_____ False_____

3. Secular humanism has no logical basis without the theory of evolution. True_____ False_____

4. What sets man, the image bearer, apart from the rest of creation is the purpose of his original design. True_____ False_____

Multiple Choice

5. Romans 1:20 says that creation
   (A) was a cosmic event of chance
   (B) proves nothing
   (C) confirms the existence of God

6. Where Darwin's theory of evolution has been the predominant view the result has been
   (A) violence
   (B) peace

(C) progress

7. The humanistic aim is to
   (A) make a better world
   (B) promote equality
   (C) rid society of the presence of the Creator by denying man is created in God's image.

8. Darwin openly taught that
   (A) all whites would eventually kill all blacks as well as other lower races
   (B) the races would eventually blend together
   (C) the races would learn to live together peaceably

Fill in the Blanks

9. Three philosophical theories that invaded the value system of both Christians and non-Christians in the twentieth century are
   (1) _____
   (2) _____
   (3) _____

10. Blindness to the basic worth of mankind prevents us from even acknowledging the _____
    _____.

11. The human frame, according to Psalm 139:14 is _____ and _____.

12. We cannot systematically debase a generation through distorted instructions and still expect them to have a healthy view of the _____. What we _____ in the classroom we _____ in the streets.

SHARPENING YOUR IMAGE—KEY BIBLE VERSES

In the space below, write three key verses from this lesson. You might also want to memorize them.

Romans 1:20
Psalm 139:14
1 John 4:20

HIGHLIGHTING YOUR IMAGE—KEY QUOTES

This generation will never settle the mystery of God as long as we ignore the mystery of man.

To devalue the creation is to deny the Creator.

The principles of evolution and special creation are opposed to one another. They will not coexist.

What we devalue in the classroom we destroy in the streets.

SHARING YOUR IMAGE— SUGGESTIONS FOR GROUP DISCUSSION

1. As a group, brainstorm and list several areas where the principles of special creation and evolution cannot coexist.

2. Have people tried to force any of the areas you listed to coexist? Discuss this.

LESSON TWO
DISCOVERING THE DIVINE DESIGN

Beginnings determine endings. Therefore, to address questions of divine design and ultimate destiny, we must look to the Bible's record of beginnings. The Book of Genesis is the seedbed for everything God has done throughout the history of man. To understand what God is presently doing today, you must discover what He initiated in the beginning. Historian Arnold Toynbee wrote, "All history, once you strip the rind off the kernel, is really spiritual."[1] The Book of Genesis reveals fundamental principles concerning God's nature. And since we are "made in the image" of our Creator—The Image Maker—we will never know our true identity, our purpose, or our destiny without an understanding of His nature.

Malachi 3:6 states, "I am the Lord, I do not change." This refers not only to His immutable character, but also to His original purpose and design for man. God's ways are perfect; they are also perfectly consistent. He has never forsaken His original mission as it is revealed in the record of creation. What God began at the genesis of earth life is still being carried out today through the power of the Holy Spirit under the administration of King Jesus.

THE MASTER ARCHITECT

You will never discover who you were meant to be if you use another person to find yourself. . . . If you want to know who you are, look at God. . . look at the Creator, not the creation.[2]

—*Myles Munroe*

Just as computer programs are designed to function efficiently and accurately when operated according to the designer's pattern, so the human race was designed according to God's divine pattern. The divine design made provision for your complete and ultimate success in life, but you have to believe it, receive it and practice it. That journey begins by discovering the wealth of potential that was programmed into God's original intention for man.

> Then God said, "Let us make human kind in our *image*, according to our *likeness*; and let them have dominion over the fish of the sea, and over the birds of the air, and over the cattle, and over all the wild animals of the earth, and over every creeping thing that creeps upon the earth." So God created humankind in his image, . . . male and female he created them. God blessed them, and God said to them, "Be fruitful and multiply, and fill the earth and subdue it; and have dominion over . . . every living thing that moves upon the earth."
> —*Genesis 1:26-28,* RSV

The Hebrew word translated as "image" is *tselem* and means "to carve" or "to cut." When applied to the creation of man in Genesis 1, *tselem* indicates that man "images" God; that is, he is a visual representation of God. The word translated as "likeness" is *demuth* and means "shape, figure, form or pattern." It was taken from a root word that means "to be like," "to resemble" or "to act like." While these words are occasionally used interchangeably, when used together they reveal a broader picture of the original design of man. This broader view has been commonly accepted throughout church history. In the second century, Irenaeus, bishop of Lyons, taught that God originally created man in His image and after His likeness. He believed that man's likeness to God, however, was lost in the Fall, whereas the image of God continued to be revealed though the whole of mankind. Only through the process of redemption could the likeness of God be restored to man.

After years of personal study, I have developed the conviction that fallen man still possesses the **image** of God, but desperately needs the atoning work of Redemption to restore him back to the **likeness** of God that he expressed before the Fall. This distinction

14

enables me to see the basic worth of all men while also recognizing the special nature of the redeemed man. Through the power of the new birth experience, Jesus Christ restores the *likeness* of God the Father back to fallen man.

ALIVE FOR THE VERY FIRST TIME

And the Lord God formed man of the dust of the ground, and breathed into his nostrils the breath of life; and man became a living soul.

—Genesis 2:7 KJV

The Bible gives us a wonderfully tender, almost maternal picture of The Image Maker leaning over Adam as He breathes into him the breath of life—as he imparts His being and nature into the first man. The first two chapters of Genesis tell us that God spoke into existence everything Adam would be able to touch, smell, feel, hear and see. Yet when it came time to create mankind, The Image Maker lovingly handcrafted him. The prophet Jeremiah and the apostle Paul both remind man in the Scriptures of his created heritage as clay on the Potter's wheel (See Jeremiah 18:1-6; Romans 9:21).

Consider the vast **difference** between this intimate, creative act and the concept of accidental evolution. The Hebrew word for the superabundant "life" that God breathed into Adam is *chayim*, which is a plural word. This is not the beginning of "multiple lives" as the reincarnationist teaches, but rather the joining of Adam's spirit, soul and body into one functioning component. God supernaturally fused these three aspects of human life together to such a degree that the Word of God is the only power capable of distinguishing between them. (See Hebrews 4:12.) When Jesus came to restore Adam's spiritually dead descendants, He called it *zoe* life because of its full abundance in essence and meaning. As the Image Maker cradled the face of Adam in His hands, He looked into his eyes with a Father's pride and said, "This is my son. He looks just like me. Not only is he created in my character, but he is also equipped to represent my conduct by managing the planet on my behalf."

Adam was created without any of the limitations with which we struggle. He was brought to life with the full knowledge and revelation of God and His majestically created order. There were no genetic flaws in his design. His brain was uncontaminated from negative thinking. His identity was undeniable, and his purpose was clear.

It is reported that Albert Einstein estimated that he used only one-third of the total capacity of his brain. If a man can suffer a two-thirds deficiency and still discover the law of relativity, what was Adam like? Without mental limitation, Adam gave names to each of the animals brought before him. While most men have an active vocabulary of four hundred words, Adam personally named thousands of animals in the Garden of Eden. I don't think we realize just how far man has fallen.

THE GENESIS OF SONSHIP

God is a father, and a father cannot be defined apart from his children. The sun, moon and stars defined Him as Creator. The earth and all its glory defined Him as Supreme Architect. The angels in all of their glory defined Him as Ancient of Days. But it took Jesus to define Him as Father. It took Adam to acknowledge him as Father. It takes you and me to receive Him as Father, And as a father, He has provided an inheritance for His children.

"So God created man in His own image . . . ." the implementation of the divine intention found in this passage introduces a number of important advancements in defining humanity. The language of this verse reveals that mankind is not the end product of an evolutionary change, but is a brand-new idea, a being produced supernaturally.

To be created in the image of God is to share in some of the characteristics of deity. Even as the wayward sons of our heavenly Father, fallen man still shares in five characteristics of the original Adamic design. These attributes are:

Man is a spirit being (Hebrews 12:9).

Man desires to interact with other spirit beings (Genesis 2:18; Psalm 63:1).

Man has the capacity to reason intellectually (Isaiah 29:24).

Man has emotional qualities (Psalm 104:15; Romans 9:2).

Man was created with the right of free choice (1 Timothy 6:9; James 4:4).

Discovering the Divine Design

COMMITTED TO THREE COVENANTS

In addition to the description of man's creation, Genesis 1:26 contains the language of covenant. God created man in the spirit of covenant. And this covenant, as with every subsequent covenant, contained an exchange of promise and responsibility. Man was created to live in covenant relationship in three dimensions: as a companion to God, in peace with other image bearers, and as a steward of creation.

Man was created to be in covenant with God. God created Adam to relate to His divine person individually, not institutionally. This pattern man, in his state of sinless innocence, was not created as a servant, but as a son—a companion of God.

As the Father of light, The Image Maker cannot fellowship with darkness. Therefore, of necessity He created man in His image and likeness. First John 1:5-7 says that God is light and in Him is no darkness at all. The most devastating consequence of sin is that it separates us from companionship with God.

Man was created to be in covenant with other men and women. In Genesis 2:18 God said, "It is not good that man should be alone; I will make him a helper companionable to him." The woman did not evolve from or grow out of the man. She was created in the image of God, out of the substance of man. Her status is not that of a second-class citizen. Eve was free to live as an image bearer. A careful study of this passage in light of the New Testament reveals that God created the man and woman redemptively equal but functionally different. The man-woman relationship implies the need for fellowship between human beings. Man was formed as a relational creature with an inherent need to be needed. Kingdom relationships frame the meaning of life.

Man was created to be in covenant with creation. Genesis 1:28 says, "God blessed them, and God said to them [*ish* and *isha*, male and female], '...have dominion....'" Adam and Eve were created to exercise joint dominion—shared responsibility. While the word "dominion" carries the idea of both authority and rule, I prefer the term "government"—the government of God. The Image Maker designed the world to be governed by mankind.

Mankind is the offspring of God. In spite of the rebellion of man and his tragic fall from grace, the image of God continues to exist upon the face of all mankind. But the **image** of God alone is not sufficient for our salvation. We must recover the beauty and power of a life lived in His **likeness**. We must begin the long journey home.

DISCOVERING YOUR IMAGE

Several principles incorporated in this lesson are listed below. In your own words, write a brief summary of each principle as you understand it. Or, if you choose, you may copy one or two statements from the lesson.

1. Beginnings determine endings.

2. "I am the Lord, I do not change," refers not only to God's immutable character, but also to his original purpose and design for mankind.

3. Mankind is created in both the image and likeness of God.

4. God is a father, and a father cannot be defined apart from his children.

5. Man was created to live in covenant relationship in three dimensions: as a companion to God, in peace with other image bearers, and as a steward of creation.

6. God created man and woman redemptively equal but functionally different.

FORMING YOUR IMAGE

The following principles are presented in a format that focuses on personal application. In the space provided after each, write what seems applicable to you.

1. Relate a personal experience where the principle of "Beginnings Determine Endings" applies to you.

2. What does it mean to you that God does not change?

3. Personalize the concept of being created in the image and likeness of God.

4. In what way, or ways, do you most relate to God as father?

5. Think about your covenant relationship to be a "companion" to God. How would you rate yourself in this relationship? (A) close and enjoyable (B) on and off (C) almost nonexistent. If this aspect of your relationship needs changing, what steps could you take to reap the benefits of this covenant relationship?

6. From your perspective as either male or female, comment on the fact that man and woman are created redemptively equal but functionally different.

REINFORCING YOUR IMAGE—PERSONAL REVIEW

True/False

1. God has never forsaken his original mission as it is revealed in the record of creation. True_____ False_____

2. God spoke Adam into existence. True_____ False_____

3. Even fallen man shares characteristics of the original Adamic design. True_____ False_____

4. Eve was not created equal to Adam. True_____ False_____

Multiple Choice

5. The likeness of God is restored to mankind through
   (A) a gradual improvement of conduct
   (B) the power of the new birth experience
   (C) church attendance and Bible study

6. Genesis 1:26-28 says that God created humankind to have dominion over
   (A) some living things
   (B) every living thing

(C) whatever he chose to

7. The words "image" and "likeness" have
   (A) exactly the same meaning
   (B) slightly different meanings
   (C) opposite meanings

8. Adam was brought to life with the
   (A) full knowledge and revelation of God
   (B) ability to develop into what God intended
   (C) desire to be like God

Fill in the Blanks

8. To address questions of divine _____ and ultimate _____, we must look to the Bible's _____ of _____.

9. Fallen man still possesses the _____ of God, but needs the atoning work of redemption to restore him back to the _____ of God.

10. Albert Einstein estimated that he used only _____ of the total capacity of his _____.

11. Man was created to be in covenant relationship with God in three dimensions: as a _____ to God, in _____ with other image bearers, and as a _____ of _____.

SHARPENING YOUR IMAGE—KEY BIBLE VERSES

In the space below, write the key Bible verses from this lesson. You might also want to memorize them.

Malachi 3:6
Genesis 1:26-28
1 John 5-7
Genesis 2:18

HIGHLIGHTING YOUR IMAGE—KEY QUOTES

Beginnings determine endings.

God is a father, and a father cannot be defined apart from his children.

The Image Maker designed the world to be governed by mankind.

SHARING YOUR IMAGE—
SUGGESTIONS FOR GROUP DISCUSSION

Explore the ramifications of the statement, "I am the Lord, I do not change."

Discuss the differences between "image" and "likeness."

LESSON THREE
THE LONG JOURNEY HOME

How far has mankind fallen? Farther than we can imagine—farther than we care to admit. We have settled for a subnormal existence—and for the most part, we are content to plod along in the status quo.

But God is not content for us to do so. He sends his prophets, his poets, and his preachers to give us glimpses of His full and complete provision. He has given us the written record not only of His creation of the heavens, the earth, and of mankind, but also of His divine purpose for His people.

It all began in the Garden. Eden was the pattern environment for the whole of the earth—a prototype of every other community that was to be constructed, structured and governed by Adam and Eve. Even as the river of Eden flowed out of the Garden carrying life to the north, south, east and west, so were Adam and Eve destined to carry the glory of God to the four corners of the planet.

Then suddenly, it all changed. Sin, in the guise of a serpent, reared its ugly head. The serpent selectively recalled the words of The Image Maker, ignoring their context and distorting their meaning. "You will be like God," the serpent told the woman, inciting desires and emotions she had never experienced before. Her curiosity gave birth to lust, and when lust was conceived, to disobedience. Adam, with eyes wide open, willingly joined her in the ultimate act of betrayal against The Image Maker. Although Adam and Eve were created in God's image and likeness, they were subject to His authority. The serpent promised that they would become coequal with God. The issue was submission. Would they yield to the authority of God's sovereign will, or would they presume to know better than God?

The fall of Adam and Eve into sin was not just an isolated act of disobedience against God, but an act of high treason against the whole of creation. The effects of sin were not confined to the "private lives" of the first family. Their personal sin had universal implications. Their sin unleashed a destructive force of unrighteousness that worked against the original design and purpose. Everything in the created order was affected by the corrosive work of sin in the earth (See Romans 8:20).

According to Multnomah professor David Needham, ". . .the biblical emphasis is on what they [Adam and Eve] lost. . . . they not only lost the hope of immortality . . . but . . . .They became alienated from the life of God" (Ephesians 3:18).[1]

A DISTORTED IMAGE

After the Fall, the image of God was not obliterated, but rather distorted. Although Adam continued to reflect a distorted **image** of the character of God, he no longer revealed the **likeness** of God. The presence of sin distorted the original image of man. A human being after the Fall, though marred by sin, is still a human being. His humanity is not reduced down to the level of a lesser primate. He is a fallen man—not a risen ape. Fallen man, at his best, is only capable of revealing brief glimpses of his former self. While revealing certain aspects of his original image, fallen man has imposed his selfish desires upon his most prominent features. Where his original image once reflected the capacity to love unselfishly, fallen man now loves when it best serves his own desire. Where his original image once reflected the righteousness of The Image Maker, fallen man now seeks to establish his righteousness apart from God. Where his original image once revealed the meaning and purpose of life, fallen man now wrestles over the reason for his existence. Where his original image once revealed unconditional acceptance, man now struggles to find his ultimate worth.

Fallen man, at his best, is only capable of revealing brief glimpses of his former self. Under the influence of unrighteousness, new emotions replaced the love, peace and joy once found in the heart of man. Romans 1:20-23 tells us that man became vain in his imagination, his foolish heart was darkened. Boasting of his personal wisdom, he became a fool, replacing the likeness of God with the actions of the evil one.

Rejected and Removed

> Then the Lord God said, "Behold, the man has become like one of Us, to know good and evil. And now, lest he put out his hand and take also of the tree of life, and eat, and live for ever"—therefore, the Lord God sent him out of the garden of Eden to till the ground from which he was taken. So He drove out the man; and He placed cherubim at the east of the garden of Eden, and a flaming sword which turned every way, to guard the way to the tree of life.
>
> —*Genesis 3:22-24*

Although he was no longer subject to the personal counsel and guidance of The Image Maker, the image bearer continued to experience the longing for his original design and purpose. He longed for companionship with his Creator; he desired meaningful interaction with other image bearers; his instinct to rule over creation was not abated. Fallen man still longs for the fulfillment of the divine intention.

On the surface, Adam's transgression may appear to be a case of rebellion rather than rejection. But to rebel against the Word of God, is, in fact, to reject God Himself. We live in a culture that attempts to piecemeal out the gospel, accepting the parts we like and rejecting the parts we don't, while maintaining friendship with God. But you can't reject the Word of God and still be His buddy. If you reject the principles of life, then your friendship with God is only a figment of your imagination.

The Principle of the Seed

Beginning with the sin of Adam in the Garden of Eden, rejection entered into the human condition and has continued to foster insecurity, isolation and intimidation in every generation since. This is the *principle of the seed* at work in the course of human history. According to this principle, you were present in the Garden, in

Adam, before you were even born. That's why the apostle Paul declares, "For as by one man's disobedience many were made sinners, so also by one Man's obedience many will be made righteous" (Romans 5:19).

We can best understand our identity in Christ by facing our identity in Adam. When we were born into this world, we were born into a kingdom, a family and a spiritual ethnicity. We had no choice in the matter. Perhaps it seems unfair that we should be judged for a sin that we didn't personally commit, in a place we've never been. But no one ever promised that life would be fair. Life isn't fair, but God is just. Even though the "seed factor" worked against us in Adam, it worked for us in Christ. We were chosen as His "spiritual seed"; we were in Him when He was crucified, buried and resurrected. Paul said, "For if by the one man's offense many died, much more the grace of God and the gift by the grace of the one Man, Jesus Christ, abounded to many" (Romans 5:15).

PERFORMANCE-BASED REJECTION

Genesis 4 contains one of the most tragic narratives in Scripture. It is the first murder in the history of mankind. But more importantly, this passage is the backdrop to every religious war that has existed since then. Cain murdered Abel over a difference of opinion concerning how God should be worshiped.

One generation removed from man's creation and complete acceptance by God, Cain was striving to gain God's favor. Fallen man digressed from *relationship-based* acceptance to *performance-based* acceptance. In the process, this first family deteriorated from being fully functional human *beings* to fully dysfunctional human *doings*. Rather than being admitted into the presence of The Image Maker based upon divine design (their essential identity), Adam's family is now struggling to be admitted based upon performance.

C. S. Lewis said that the Fall was not mere deterioration, but a loss of status as a species. A new species, never made by God, had sinned its way into existence.[2]

Genesis 5:1-3 ". . . When Adam had lived one hundred and thirty years, he became the father of a son in his own likeness, according to his image, and named him Seth." Adam's son Seth bore the image and likeness of Adam in his fallen state. Again we see the use of both the words *image* and *likeness*. Not only was Seth born with the physical characteristics of his father, he also carried his father's propensity to act in a certain manner. Adam's "fallenness" was spiritually and genetically transferred to the next generation. The likeness of God was perfect. The likeness of Adam was imperfect. The likeness of God was righteous. The likeness of Adam was unrighteousness. Every living being upon the face of this planet now bears the likeness of fallen man.

The cycle of dysfunctionalism continues from one generation to the next. God chose a grace-filled man by the name of Noah and destroyed the original environment that contained the rejection of Adam and Eve. Yet Noah still struggled with the issue of acceptance and rejection because of the human condition into which he had been born. Noah was several generations removed from Adam, yet the sin continued on. In spite of the newly renovated earth, the force of rejection was still present, because sin is not a product of environment.

You can be born into the most loving and nurturing environment and still struggle with issues of acceptance and affirmation, because rejection has been built into your genetic makeup. Rejection is a human condition. Wherever you find humans, you will find men and women struggling with the issues of identity, affirmation, self-worth and acceptance.

A Vital Discovery

Mistaken identity always results in a wrong behavior—a behavior out of accord with one's true identity. For example, if you can convince a man that he is a slave—when in fact he is a king by birth—then he will develop a slave mentality and live far beneath his inherited right. He will never rise to the throne because he believed a lie concerning his identity. Who you are determines how you act.

Long before the language of "self-esteem" ever worked its way into the pop-psychology culture, the Bible identified the principle of self-image as the key to fulfilling one's destiny. The wisest man who lived phrased it this way: "For as he [man] thinks in his heart, so is he" (Proverbs 23:7).

We have settled for a subnormal existence. In reality, we do not know just how far man has fallen, but we do have the road map back to full restoration. We are in the process of rediscovering whom and what God originally designed us to be. God will someday have a generation (the generation of the last Adam) that will ultimately repair and rebuild everything forfeited and destroyed by the first Adam. It all began in the Garden, and it is destined to end with some generation. Why not let it be ours?

DISCOVERING YOUR IMAGE

Several principles incorporated in this lesson are listed below. In your own words, write a brief summary of each principle as you understand it. Or, if you choose, you may copy one or two statements from the lesson.

1. How far has mankind fallen? Farther than we can imagine or care to admit.

2. After the Fall of man, the image of God was not obliterated, but rather distorted.

3. Fallen man digressed from a relationship-based acceptance to a performance-based acceptance.

4. Adam's fallenness was spiritually and genetically transferred to the next generation.

5. Mistaken identity always results in wrong behavior—with behavior out of accord with one's true identity.

6. We have settled for a subnormal existence. But we are in the process of rediscovering whom and what God originally designed us to be.

FORMING YOUR IMAGE

The following principles are presented in a format that focuses on personal application. In the space provided after each, write what seems applicable to you.

1. Why do you think it is so difficult for us to admit how far mankind has fallen from God's original design and purpose?

2. List one or two ways in which you are aware that the image of God is distorted in humankind.

3. Honestly examine your relationship with God, particularly looking for areas where you have allowed your performance to be the criteria for your relationship.

4. Personalize how Adam's fallenness spiritually and genetically affects you.

5. Give a personal example of how mistaken identity results in wrong behavior.

6. In what areas have you settled for a subnormal existence? What steps can you take on the journey to rediscover whom and what God designed you to be?

REINFORCING YOUR IMAGE—PERSONAL REVIEW

True/False

1. The serpent quoted God's words out of context and distorted them when he enticed Eve to disobey God.
   True_____ False_____

2. Adam and Eve's sin only affected their generation.
   True_____ False_____

3. A human being after the fall is reduced to the level of a lesser primate. True_____ False_____

4. Fallen man still longs for the companionship of his Creator.
   True_____ False_____

Multiple Choice

5. The corrosive work of sin in the earth affected
   (A) only the human race
   (B) only the human race and the animal kingdom
   (C) everything in the created order

6. After the fall the image of God in man was
    (A) obliterated
    (B) still the same
    (C) distorted

7. Cain murdered Abel over
    (A) a woman
    (B) an inheritance
    (C) a difference of opinion in how God should be worshiped

8. After the flood, in a newly cleansed environment, mankind
    (A) still struggled with the issue of acceptance and rejection
    (B) lived holier lives
    (C) began to please God

Fill in the Blanks

9. Where man's original image once revealed the_____
    and _____ of life, fallen man now wrestles
    over the reason for his _____.

10. Even though the "seed factor" worked _____ us in
    _____, it _____ _____ us in _____.

11. Fallen man digressed from _____ - _____ accep-
    tance to _____ - _____ acceptance.

12. Mistaken identity always results in a _____
    _____ , a behavior out of accord with one's
    _____.

SHARPENING YOUR IMAGE—KEY BIBLE VERSES

In the space below, write the key Bible verses from this lesson. You
might also want to memorize them.

Romans 8:20
Romans 1:20-23

Romans 5:15
Genesis 5:13
Genesis 3:22-24
Proverbs 23:7

HIGHLIGHTING YOUR IMAGE—KEY QUOTES

We have settled for a subnormal existence.

You can't reject the Word of God and still be His buddy.

Life isn't fair, but God is just.

Mistaken identity always results in a wrong behavior.

Who you are determines how you act.

SHARING YOUR IMAGE— SUGGESTIONS FOR GROUP DISCUSSION

1. Explore the statement, "We live in a culture that attempts to piecemeal out the gospel, accepting parts we like and rejecting parts we don't. List some commonly held truths most of us accept; then list some many people reject. Discuss why this is.

2. As a group, brainstorm and list as many varieties of performance-based religion as you can. Then discuss why men and women so readily accept this distortion of God's ways.

LESSON FOUR
BACK TO EDEN AND BEYOND

There is a radical difference between the way you were originally created and the way you were finally born. The Image Maker originally designed you to live in righteousness, but you were "born in sin and shaped in iniquity." The apostle Paul describes our condition this way, "Therefore, just as through one man sin entered the world, and death through sin, and thus death spread to all men, because all sinned" (Romans 5:12). And in Ephesians 2:1, he said that mankind was "dead in trespasses and sins."

To be spiritually dead is to be alienated from the life source of heaven. And in this alienation, man is open to the contaminated waters of counterfeit life presented by the usurper, Satan. This perverted association became man's defining agency, so when Jesus looked at Adam's spiritually dead descendants, He said, "You are of your father the devil, and the desires of your father you want to do" (John 8:44).

Perhaps the clearest Scripture defining the relationship of fallen man to Satan is Ephesians 2:3. Paul describes mankind by saying, "We . . . were by nature children of wrath." We existed without any meaningful relationship to the Father of creation. Notice the paradox: fallen man *lives*, "*dead* in trespasses and sins." How can one be both alive and dead at the same time? It is possible because man is disconnected from the true origin of life and reconnected to pseudo life. In our blindness to the original design, we settled for a counterfeit form of existence.

To reinstate the image bearer to his original condition in the image and likeness of God, man needed to be reborn. The Son of God was sent from heaven to open up a spiritual birth canal through which we might be born from above. Through the miracle of spiritual regeneration, Jesus made us to be our *true* selves. Only as we "live and move and find our being in Him" will we discover who we were really meant to be. Our identity is clearly linked to His existence in the world.

Jesus said "Except a man be born again, he cannot see the kingdom of God" (John 3:33). Jesus was proposing something far greater than the vague, symbolic ritual commonly required of those converting to Judaism or even some pagan religion. He was speaking of an actual, revolutionary change in man's essential being. Jesus used the Greek phrase *gennao anothen*, which can be translated literally as "born from above." This is the supernatural process that brings us back to Eden and beyond.

- You were born the first time by the will of man, but the second time by the will of God.
- The first birth formed you in the image of God, but the second birth formed you in His likeness.
- The first birth created you by the blood of man; the second birth created you by the blood of Jesus Christ.

In order to enter the kingdom, man must become a different "spiritual species." Professor David Needham, in his book, *Birthright*, describes the spiritual parallel found between physical conception and birth and the new birth process.

By physical conception my parents gave me a "flesh" birth. It involved much more than my *getting* something. I *became* someone. I became a real, full-fledged, *flesh* person. Similarly, by the new birth, I *became a brand-new kind of person.* Jesus did not say being born again equals *getting* the Holy Spirit. He said it equaled *becoming* spirit.[1]

Spiritual regeneration is not some type of religious appendage that God attaches to your old nature. It is the transformation of the old man into The Image Maker's new creation. It is the radical reconstruction of a person's essential identity.

THE LAW OF REPRODUCTION

Everything in the created order was designed to reproduce after its own kind, according to Genesis 1. This "law of reproduction" even extended to the creation of man, when The Image Maker said, "Let us make man in our image, according to our likeness" (Genesis 1:26). Just as dogs cannot produce cats, nor cats produce dogs, so the flesh cannot produce spirit, nor the spirit produce flesh.

In His role as the last Adam, Jesus came to restore the likeness of God back to the image bearer. This is a full and complete conversion resulting in the regeneration of man. Paul put it this way:

> Therefore, if anyone is in Christ, he is a new creation; old things have passed away; behold, all things have become new.
>
> *—2 Corinthians 5:17*

You are, as the new creation, who you are whether you understand it or not, believe it or not or even act like it or not! When you surrendered your life to Jesus Christ, you were instantaneously reborn, regenerated, re-created, renewed and spiritually re-coded.

THE REDUCTION OF CHRISTIANITY

I emphasize the fact of our new creation identity in Christ so strongly because far too many Christians have reduced the new birth experience down to the level of a self-improvement program. We have fallen for the self-esteem trap rather than standing confident in our self-worth.

I believe the greatest danger we face in the North American church is not over the *seduction* of Christianity but in the *reduction* of Christianity. I sincerely doubt if many genuine, Bible-believing Christians are in danger of renouncing their belief in the virgin birth of Christ or His physical, literal, bodily return. But scores of believers are confused as to the radical nature of the new birth experience. We have settled for a watered-down version of authentic New Testament Christianity.

I am shocked by the number of born-again believers who lack an understanding of their essential identity in Christ. Mistaken identity always results in behavior out of accord with one's true identity. When we are uncertain about our identity, our mission is obscured. The dominion mandate is not being exercised by many who fill our church buildings today because they have settled for a distorted image of their ultimate worth and value.

While society both needs and benefits from various reform movements and programs, we cannot equate Christianity with them. The new birth experience is not about being "reformed," it is about being spiritually "re-formed." Instead of accepting the lie of "once a sinner, always a sinner," we must come to believe that we truly "passed from death unto life" and "all things have been made new." The church was not designed to serve as a support group for those who are attempting to gradually become Christian one day at a time. Spiritual regeneration is not a progressive experience. The new birth is not offered on the installment program. It is an instantaneous miracle.

You can use psychology to dig in the ashes of your former self, but remember that your former self was "crucified with Christ" and no longer exists. You can use distorted theology in an attempt to resurrect your former self, but heaven will not cooperate with your deformed perception. The good news is that you have been permanently altered at the core of your being.

The sum total of the Christian life was purchased for you on the cross of Calvary. Spiritually you have been given everything you need for the journey toward the "measure of the stature and fullness of Christ." Tragically, many Christians are still waiting to possess what the cross legally gave us.

AN IDENTITY CHANGE

The apostle Paul could not have said it more clearly:

> I am crucified with Christ: nevertheless I live; yet not I, but Christ liveth in me: and the life which I now life in the flesh I live by the faith of the Son of God, who loved me, and gave himself for me.
>
> —*Galatians 2:20*, KJV

Jesus Christ became what He was not so that we might become what we were not. As He was crucified for our sins, He was made sin so that we might be made righteous. This is the divine exchange between God and man. This exchange transforms us into a brand-new identity.

How to Become Complete

Only one person in the universe is capable of completing you. You will never find completeness in your husband, wife or any other earthly relationship. The Fall of Adam left you with an inherent desire to be "completed" by God alone. One Christian songwriter called this a "God-sized hole in every one of us." My generation's experimentation with drugs, alcohol and sexual promiscuity has been nothing more than self-medication. This is man's attempt to prescribe a remedy to fill his inner longing apart from faith in Jesus Christ.

Through the incredible gift of God's own Son, we are spiritually transformed and eternally complete. Only Jesus can fill the deepest longing of your heart. Only Jesus can repair your broken self-image. If you want to understand whom God originally created you to be, go back and research the life of Adam before the Fall. After you have developed a picture of Adam in his state of innocent righteousness, continue your study with the life of Jesus Christ. As the pattern Son, Jesus reveals the standard for our personhood and also for living life. We need to make the journey back to Eden and beyond. This process is only possible through the life, death and resurrection of the last Adam, who came to make things right.

DISCOVERING YOUR IMAGE

Several principles incorporated in this lesson are listed below. In your own words, write a brief summary of each principle as you understand it. Or, if you choose, you may copy one or two statements from the lesson.

1. There is a radical difference in the way you were originally created and the way you were finally born.

2. Through the miracle of spiritual regeneration, Jesus made us to be our true selves.

3. You are, as the new creation, who you are whether you understand it or not, believe it or not or even act like it or not.

4. The greatest danger we face in the North American church is not the "seduction" of Christianity, but the "reduction" of Christianity.

5. Jesus Christ became what He was not (sin), in order to make us what we were not (righteous).

6. Only one person in the universe is capable of completing you. Only Jesus can fill the deepest longing of your heart.

FORMING YOUR IMAGE

The following principles are presented in a format that focuses on personal application. In the space provided after each, write what seems applicable to you.

1. Contrast several characteristics of mankind's original created condition and the condition in which all men and women are born.

2. In light of what Jesus did for you in spiritual regeneration, how would you describe your "true self"?

3. Personalize the statement, "I (your name) am a new creation," and discuss what that means to you.

4. Give an example (or several) of how the church today has "reduced" Christianity.

5. What does it mean to you personally that "Jesus Christ became what he was not in order to make you what you were not."

6. Have you experienced the "completeness" only found in Jesus Christ? Yes_____ No_____. Explain.

REINFORCING YOUR IMAGE—PERSONAL REVIEW

True/False

1. To be spiritually dead is to be alienated from the life source of heaven. True_____ False_____

2. Even though a man is born again, he is still a sinner. True_____ False_____

3. Spiritual regeneration is an instantaneous miracle. True_____ False_____

4. The flesh cannot produce spirit, but the spirit can produce flesh. True_____ False_____

Multiple Choice

5. To reinstate the image bearer to his original condition in the image and likeness of God man needed
   (A) punishment and correction
   (B) to be reborn
   (C) detailed instructions
6. Spiritual regeneration is
   (A) a religious appendage God attaches to your nature

(B) the transformation of the "old man" into the new creation

(C) accomplished through self-improvement

7. The sum total of the Christian life
   (A) was purchased for you on the cross of Calvary
   (B) will only be obtainable in heaven
   (C) can only be experienced in church

8. The only person in the universe capable of completing you is
   (A) your spouse
   (B) your children
   (C) Jesus Christ

Fill in the Blanks

9. There is a radical difference between the way you were
   _____ _____ and the way you were
   _____ _____.

10. Everything in the created order was designed to
    _____ after its _____ _____.

11. Jesus Christ became what He _____ _____ so that we
    might become what we _____ _____.

12. The fall of Adam left you with an inherent desire to be
    _____ by God.

STRENGTHENING YOUR IMAGE—KEY BIBLE VERSES

In the space below write the key Bible verses from this lesson. You
might also want to memorize them.

Romans 5:12
John 8:44
John 3:33
2 Corinthians 5:17
Galatians 2:20

HIGHLIGHTING YOUR IMAGE—KEY QUOTES

There is a radical difference in the way you were originally created and the way you were finally born.

You are, as the new creation, who you are whether you understand it or not, believe it or not, or even act like it.

Jesus Christ became what He was not so that we might become what we were not.

Spiritual regeneration is not a progressive experience . . . It is an instantaneous miracle.

SHARING YOUR IMAGE—
SUGGESTIONS FOR GROUP DISCUSSION

1. Discuss how everything in the created order was designed to reproduce after its own kind.

2. Discuss some of man's attempts to fill the inner longing that can only be filled by God.

PART II:
DISCOVERING YOUR IDENTITY

LESSON FIVE
AWAKEN TO RIGHTEOUSNESS

New Covenant righteousness is far more than appropriate Christian conduct. Under the Law of Moses, righteousness was simply a matter of appropriate conduct. The law centered on man's behavior rather than his heart attitude. A man could outwardly obey the rules while harboring resentment, lust, bitterness, hate, etc. in his heart. The classic illustration of this is the little boy who was corrected by his mother and sent to sit in the corner as punishment for his disobedience. With eyes glaring defiance, he physically obeyed the law of his mother. Later, his mother heard him mutter from his chair in the corner, "I may be sitting down on the outside, but I'm standing up on the inside." While the Law of Moses compelled man to "sit down on the outside," it had no power to change the heart attitude.

The Hebrew word for righteousness is *tsadaq*, and cannot be adequately expressed or translated by any one English word. It means "stiff or straight"; in a spiritual sense, *tsadaq* implies a full weight or measure toward God; it is also used in the sense of rendering justice and making wrongs right. The Greek word for righteousness is *dikaiosune* and means "equity of character."

Both words convey the concept of a standard of weights and measures as they have to do with righteousness. The following natural example helps to clarify this concept. The National Institute of Standards and Technology determines the criteria for all weights and measures in the United States (i.e., a pound is 16 ounces; a foot is 12 inches). Individual interpretation or variation is not allowed; no grocer can say, "In my store a pound is 14 ounces." No mayor can say, "In our city, a foot actually means 20 inches." Any variations of the official definition of an ounce, pound, foot, etc. is a federal offense. The legal qualifications have been set and are not subject to personal interpretation.

In a spiritual sense, the Law of Moses contained the weights-and-measures standard for almighty God. It defined, on God's terms, what a full measure of righteousness was. The Law defined the standard of conduct by which the whole earth was to be judged.

In the Old Testament, the matter of righteousness was always related to Jehovah, His Word, His character and His actions. Men were only referred to as "righteous" when their lives exhibited these same godly characteristics.

PERFORMANCE-BASED RIGHTEOUSNESS

Old Covenant righteousness was performance-based righteousness. Like the modern-day concept of self-esteem, man's righteousness (worth and value) fluctuated from day to day based upon his accomplishment. The tragedy with performance-based righteousness is that even if you succeed in keeping 99 percent of the Law, you still fail. You are condemned before the holiness of God, because "for whoever shall keep the whole law, and yet stumble in one point, he is guilty of all" (James 2:10).

None of us are brazen enough to think that we can stand before the throne of almighty God based upon our good behavior and call that a full measure of righteousness. Yes, our good behavior may result in a form (or degree) of righteousness, but it isn't a full measure. It does not meet God's weights-and-measures standard. The apostle Paul put it this way:

> For they being ignorant of God's righteousness, and seeking to establish their own righteousness, have not submitted to the righteousness of God.
>
> —*Romans 10:3*

The righteousness that is of the Law engages man in a life-and-death struggle for freedom—with the inadequate weapons of sheer force and determination. The result is a few partial and temporary victories and numerous defeats. The cycle is vicious: We try . . . we fail . . . we despair . . . we confess our sin and failure . . . experience brief flashes of hope . . . and we try . . . we fail . . . we despair. There has to be a better way! There is. Paul describes it:

> For *what the law could not do* in that it was weak through
> the flesh, *God did* by sending His own Son in the likeness
> of sinful flesh, on account of sin: He condemned sin in the
> flesh, that the righteous requirement of the law might be
> fulfilled in us who do not walk according to the flesh but
> according to the Spirit.
>
> —*Romans 8:3-4* (emphasis added)

When we struggle to clothe ourselves in the righteousness of our
own good works, we are consigned to stand before the holiness of
God in filthy rags rather than in the beauty in which He has clothed
us. Isaiah 64:6 declares that "all our righteousness [the righteousness that comes about by the law] are like filthy rags."

THE ONLY RIGHTEOUS MAN

Because fallen man could not accomplish the standard required
by the Law, The Image Maker sent His only begotten Image Bearer
to earth to fulfill the divine requirement. The Father did everything
He could to ensure mankind's reintegration into His spiritual family
through sending His Son, Jesus, to die as the sacrifice needed to
reconnect The Image Maker with His wayward children on the
earth.

Jesus fulfilled the Law as a human being, not as a divine being.
He kept the Law as the "Son of Man" and fulfilled the righteous
demands of almighty God. That's why He declared in Matthew
5:17, "Do not think that I came to destroy the Law or the Prophets.
I did not come to destroy but to fulfill."

Jesus fulfilled the Law out of the motive of pure love in order to
offer us the full measure of righteousness, which He secured
through His obedience. It is impossible for God to accept any other
righteousness than that which Jesus Christ offered to Him. No other
man ever met the full requirements. Under the New Covenant there
is now only one standard of weights and measures for perfect righteousness—the life of the Lord Jesus Christ.

NEW COVENANT RIGHTEOUSNESS

New Covenant righteousness is the righteousness that comes

through faith. Paul writes in Philippians 3:8-9 ". . . not having mine own righteousness, which is of the law, but that which is through the faith of Christ, the righteousness which is of God by faith."

New Covenant righteousness is not a result of what you perform, but of who you become—in Christ you become a new creation. The key to New Covenant righteousness is contained in this simple principle: When a man is found in Christ, he is judged righteous before God the Father. True righteousness is only found in one place, and that is "in Christ."

David Needham makes the following comment:

"At the risk of oversimplification the difference between Old Covenant righteousness and New Covenant righteousness can be compared to the difference between "God as my helper" and "God as my life."[1]

BECOMING A RIGHTEOUS MAN

New Covenant righteousness flows out of your identity as the new creation.

> Therefore if any man be in Christ, he is a new creature: old things are passed away; behold, all things are become new....For he hath *made* him to be sin for us, who knew no sin; that we might be *made* the righteousness of God in him.
> —*2 Corinthians 5:17, 21,* KJV, emphasis added

Paul the Apostle declares that the new creation is formed out of the righteousness of God's own character. He is not simply clothed in the righteousness of Christ, but the very ingredient that now makes up his essential identity is God's own righteousness.

Philip Yancey made this observation:

> "This unfathomable idea of identity exchange is implicit in conversion....we carry within us not just the image of, or the philosophy of, or faith in, but the actual substance of God....the spiritual genes of Christ: as we stand before God, we are judged on the basis of Christ's perfection, not our unworthiness."[2]

Consider this awesome concept: *To the degree that He was made sin, you were made righteous!* He became what He was not, in order that you might become what you were not. Jesus never committed or practiced sin. He was made sin. In like manner, you are not righteous because you practice righteousness. You are righteous because you were *made* to be righteous. We dare not water down this principle to appease those who are satisfied with their limited understanding of the atoning work of Jesus Christ.

Your righteousness is predicated upon the fact that Jesus was made to be sin. If you weren't really made righteous, then Jesus was never made to be sin, and the whole truth of redemption is in jeopardy. You cannot have one without the other!

Consider that Jesus was made to be every heinous sin that ever crossed the perverted mind of fallen man. As disturbing as it may seem, He carried the sins of rape, incest and infanticide to the cross. Jesus willingly allowed the vilest of sins to be placed upon Him in His suffering. While hanging on the cross, this pure Man who never committed one single sin suddenly felt the overwhelming pressure of the depraved nature of sin. He carried the past, present and future sins of man with Him to the cross, nailing them to the tree, securing eternal freedom for those who put their trust in Him. I cannot overemphasize that the degree to which He was made to be sin is the same degree that you were made to be righteous.

WHO IS YOUR SOURCE?

New Covenant righteousness is about our dependence upon the Father to keep our righteousness secure through His covenant with the Son. As we share the life of the Son, we are entitled to the same measure of righteousness that He secured through His perfect obedience to the Law of Moses.

This dependence will lead to righteous acts of obedience, but the source is our relationship with the Father—not our good works. Our *doing* flows from our *being*. The new creation does the works of righteousness because he *has been made* righteous, not in order to *become* righteous.

Jesus understood the secret of absolute dependence upon the Father. As the Son of Man, he was completely dependent upon the Father to nourish Him with the life of heaven. That's why He said, "I can of Mine own self do nothing!" (See John 8:28.) Jesus did not perform miracles as a divine being. He performed them as a mere man anointed by God. Acts 10:38 says, "God anointed Jesus of Nazareth with the Holy Spirit and with power, who went about doing good and healing all who were oppressed by the devil, for God was with Him."

God has also anointed us (His spiritually regenerated children) with the Holy Spirit and with power. We are who God has declared us to be—we are the righteousness of God in Christ Jesus. God did much more than separate us from the deformity of sin; He re-formed us in the image of righteousness.

I believe that the church has majored on behavior modification when we should focus on identity revelation. The Image Maker has created us to be His Image Bearers—to be lights in a darkened world. Let's believe God. Let's embrace that we are what He says we are. Let's awaken to righteousness.

DISCOVERING YOUR IMAGE

Several principles incorporated in this lesson are listed below. In your own words, write a brief summary of each principle as you understand it. Or if you choose, you may copy one or two statements from the book.

1. Under the law of Moses, righteousness was simply a matter of appropriate conduct.

2. Old Covenant righteousness was performance-based righteousness.

3. The righteousness that is of the Law engages us in a life and death struggle for freedom.

4. True righteousness is only found in one place in the universe—and that is "in Christ."

5. Your righteousness is predicated upon the fact that Jesus was made to be sin.

6. New Covenant righteousness is about our dependence upon the Father to keep our righteousness secure through his covenant with the Son.

FORMING YOUR IMAGE

The following principles are presented in a format that focuses on personal application. In the space provided after each, write what seems applicable to you.

1. Give a personal example of doing something which appeared righteous while your heart attitude was not right.

2. List 2 or 3 examples of performance based righteousness in your life (past or present).

3. Give a personal example of how you have fought the losing battle of trying to establish your own righteousness.

4. What does it mean to you that true righteousness is only found in Christ.

5. Personalize how Jesus was **made** to be sin—think of Him on the cross and picture your specific sins being laid upon Him. Then picture how He dealt with them.

6. Are you depending on your heavenly Father to keep you secure in New Covenant righteousness? Explain.

REINFORCING YOUR IMAGE—PERSONAL REVIEW

True/False

1. New Covenant incorporates trusting Jesus and obeying all the law of Moses. True_____ False_____

2. True righteousness flows out of your identity as the new creation. True_____ False_____

3. Jesus said that He came to destroy and do away with the Law. True_____ False_____

4. Jesus was made to be every heinous sin that ever crossed the perverted mind of man. True_____ False_____

Multiple Choice

5. New Covenant Righteousness is the righteousness that comes through
   (A) joining a church
   (B) faith
   (C) the law

6. Paul declares that the new creation is formed out of
   (A) clay
   (B) God's breath
   (C) the righteousness of God's own character

7. The new creation does the works of righteousness
   (A) in order to become righteousness
   (B) because he wants to appear righteous
   (C) because he has been made righteous

8. Our righteousness under the New Covenant is kept secure through
   (A) our covenant with God
   (B) our covenant with the church
   (C) God's covenant with the Son

Fill in the Blanks

9. Jesus fulfills the Law as a _____ being, not as a _____ being.

10. New Covenant righteousness is not a result of what you _____, but of _____ you _____.

11. To the degree that Jesus was _____ _____, you were _____ _____.

12. I believe the church has majored in _____ _____, when we should focus on _____ _____.

STRENGTHENING YOUR IMAGE—KEY BIBLE VERSES

In the space below write the key Bible verses from this lesson. You might also want to memorize them.

Romans 10:3
James 2:10
Romans 8:3-4
Isaiah 64:6
Matthew 5:17
Philippians 3:8-9
2 Corinthians 5:17, 21
John 8:28

HIGHLIGHTING YOUR IMAGE—KEY QUOTES

New Covenant righteousness is far more than appropriate Christian conduct.

Old Covenant righteousness was performance-based.

To the degree that Jesus was made sin, you were made righteous.

The church has majored on behavior modification when we should focus on identity revelation.

SHARING YOUR IMAGE— SUGGESTIONS FOR GROUP DISCUSSION

1. In your group discussion, take ten minutes and brainstorm every practice or code of conduct that you (or other Christians) have used to try and become righteous. Have one person in your group write these down as they are mentioned. Then discuss where you think most of these ideas came from. Also, discuss what kind of results they produce.

2. Consider the statement, "Jesus was made to be every sin (whether small, large, or in between) known to mankind."

Then have one member of the group list all the sins the group can think of that were placed on Jesus. What's your reaction to that?

LESSON SIX
BECOMING WHO YOU ALREADY ARE

Christian growth is the process of becoming who you already are. Millions of people are born again by the will of God and have the right to become fully matured sons and daughters, but they never go on to maturity because they lack a proper understanding of their essential identity in Christ. Our spiritual perception always determines our final destination. If we perceive the new birth experience to be the final destination in life, then we will settle for something less than our full potential in the kingdom of God.

> Behold, what manner of love the Father hath bestowed upon us, that we should be called the sons of God . . . Beloved, now are we the sons of God, and it doth not yet appear what we shall be: but we know that when he shall appear, we shall be like him . . . .
>
> *—1 John 31-2*

A noticeable tension exists between the phrases: "*now* are we the sons of God" and "it doth *not yet* appear." John is showing us that our *identity* is a settled fact, but our spiritual *maturity* is yet to be determined. Anyone who has ever parented children is aware of the vast difference between an immature son and one who is fully developed in those things pertaining to his destiny.

Following the miracle of spiritual regeneration, there is nothing you can do to become any more of a son of God than what you have already done. You can become a *mature* son, an *obedient* son, and a *faithful* son—but you are already a *son* of God.

Consider your natural birth. Who you are (your gender) is determined at the moment of conception; nine months later that identity of either male or female is evident. You were genetically constructed as a male or female; there is no "in between" category. However, throughout your life you can choose educational, emotional and physical activities that can either enhance or detract from your "maleness" or your "femininity," but no activity will alter your essential identity.

For example, working out three times each week at a health club may make me a strong man, but I am already male. Completing my Ph.D., may make me an educated man, but I am already male. Likewise, you may enhance and develop your identity as a son of God, but you are already a son! Nothing you can do after the new birth can make you any more of a son.

Many Christians are engaged in a life-or-death struggle to become who they already are in Christ. Failing to perceive the reality of their new identity, they continue the search to discover what they have already become. When I speak of becoming who you already are, I am describing the process by which you come to terms with who you are in Christ.

If an outward change in our appearance took place when we were born again, perhaps it would be easier for us to accept who we are. The evidence would be there for us, and others, to see. But "faith is the evidence of things not seen"—so said the writer of Hebrews. And faith is the principle by which God has chosen to reveal Himself to mankind. God's Word declares that we are new creations—sons of God. It's up to us to believe His Word.

The Image Maker has already deposited everything in you, through His incorruptible seed, that you will ever need to become who you already are in Christ. Second Peter 1:3 says, "According as his divine power hath given unto us all things that pertain unto life and godliness. . ." (KJV) J.B. Phillips' translation of 1 Peter 1:23 is fascinating: "For you are not just mortals now but sons of God; the live, permanent Word of the living God has given you his own indestructible heredity."

Consider this: Mankind is the only aspect of creation that struggles with its identity. The birds, bees, dogs and fleas do not give the issue of identity a second thought. An apple sapling never struggles with an identity crisis, desperate to become an apple tree. The genetic structure of that apple tree is designed and destined for one thing—to produce fruit after its own kind. With the exception of mankind, God's entire kingdom is at peace with its inherent design and ultimate destiny. In all of creation only mankind has "fallen" from its divine design and destiny.

GROWING INTO YOUR IDENTITY

Christian growth is the process of becoming who we already are in Christ. And while it is possible to take part in various religious activities and functions in an effort to demonstrate who we are, unless we build on the sure foundation of who God says we are in Christ, our efforts will never produce God's intended results.

The wonderful thing about this "becoming process" is that we have all of God's grace at our disposal. Romans 4 tells us that Abraham was first "named" father and then "became" a father because he dared to trust God to do what only God could do—raise the dead to life. Because God "named" us the new creation, we have all the grace to manifest new creation realities—personally, prophetically, practically. What a difference in attempting to *manufacture* a life in Christ through duty and self-denial and in *living* in the awe of a magnificent obsession to simply become who we already are.

The question that comes to mind is this: Why does the Father call us to spiritual maturity? If getting to heaven is the only thing that matters, then why grow up? Why spend so much time praying and studying God's Word if it produces no personal profit? Who wants to suffer through unnecessary growing pains? I believe these questions reveal the crux of the matter. The primary reason why so many people say the sinner's prayer, walk away from the altar and never go on to discipleship is because they have never been shown the value of growing up into Christ in all things. There are many reasons we have been called to grow spiritually, but the foremost reason is this: Only the fully mature son can inherit everything the Father has willed to him. Romans 8:14 declares, "For as many as are led by the Spirit of God, these are the sons [the fully matured sons] of God." The goal of the Holy Spirit is to prepare you for your spiritual inheritance.

Part of that preparation includes correction through chastening.

The writer of Hebrews said, "My son, do not despise the chastening of the Lord, nor be discouraged when you are rebuked by Him; for whom the Lord loves He chastens . . . If you are without chastening . . . then you are illegitimate, and not sons."—Hebrews 12:5-9

When I was a child my father chastened me. I now realize, being a father myself, that it was true when he said, "This is going to hurt me worse than it hurts you." Chastening produces boundaries and safeguards that enable us to live long enough to grow up. Volumes could be written about the wretched condition, the premature deaths, and the overall disillusionment of a generation whose earthly parents have failed to correct them.

REVELATION PRODUCES REVOLUTION

Renewing our minds to the knowledge of our identity in Christ takes more than factual information; it necessitates spiritual revelation. Proverbs 23:7 declares that "as [a man] thinks in his heart, so is he." Long before that familiar line worked its way into Psychology 101, the Bible identified it as a spiritual principle. The secret to living the new creation life is to renew our minds to new creation realities. We literally program our minds with the revelation that will ultimately set us free. Information will not set you free, but revelation will.

Many Christians have failed to discern the vast difference between truth and revelation. Let me explain it to you like this: Truth doesn't require a personal application to be true, but revelation cannot exist independently of a personal application. Revelation is actually the truth that you and I have received and applied.

When paraphrasing John 8:31, the Jerusalem Bible says, "Your mind must be renewed by a spiritual revolution." The object of a revolution is to overthrow "governmental authority." If your mind has been ruled by the "governmental authority" of the kingdom of darkness, you can dethrone its power by renewing your mind to the truth of God's Word.

CASTING DOWN THE WRONG IMAGE

In ancient days when cities were built within massive walls, in order for an enemy to take the city, three objectives had to be accomplished: (1) scale or penetrate the wall, (2) invade the towers where the lookouts were stationed, (3) capture the men of military strategy. The apostle Paul used military terminology to illustrate how our minds become the strongholds of darkness and what must be accomplished to gain freedom. Second Corinthians 10 speaks of pulling down strongholds, casting down imaginations, and every high thing that exalts itself against the knowledge of God, and of bringing every thought into captivity and obedience of Christ.

Any teaching, belief, or tradition that contradicts who the Bible says you are in Christ must be cast down. The enemy fights us every step of the way in this process because he knows you will never discover your true authority until you first discover your true identity. And when you live and walk in the true authority of your new creation identity, Satan can find no "place" in your life.

Even though the light of the glorious gospel has set us free, the enemy still attempts to operate through the strongholds that he has established. He seeks to rule our lives through the habits we established when we were under his control. The real battleground is at the point of the stronghold—the thing we fall back under when pressure comes upon us. Many Christians still hide under the stronghold of personal addiction. They bow their knees to the ruling power of gluttony, alcohol, nicotine, sex, anger, withdrawal, and so forth because they do not know who they really are.

Inherent within your essential identity exists the capacity to behave accordingly. If you do not understand your identity as a son or daughter of the kingdom, then you will live your entire life beneath the privileges of your sonship. Do you know who you are? Do you fully perceive whom God made you to be in Christ Jesus? The loving heart of The Image Maker beats with the desire for you to comprehend who He has created you to be.

DISCOVERING YOUR IMAGE

Several principles incorporated in this lesson are listed below. In your own words, write a brief summary of each principle as you understand it. Or if you choose, you may copy one or two statements from the book.

1. Millions of people are born again by the will of God and have the right to become fully matured sons and daughters, but they never go on to maturity because they lack a proper understanding of their essential identity in Christ.

2. Following the miracle of spiritual regeneration, there is nothing you can do to become any more of a son of God than what you have already done.

3. The Image Maker has already deposited everything in you, through His incorruptible seed, that you will ever need to become who you already are in Christ.

4. Only the fully mature son can inherit everything the Father has willed to him.

5. Many Christians have failed to discern the vast difference between truth and revelation.

6. You will never discover your true authority until you first discover your true identity.

FORMING YOUR IMAGE

The following principles are presented in a format that focuses on personal application. In the space provided after each, write what seems applicable to you.

1. Do you think you have a proper understanding of who you are in Christ? Yes____ No____ Explain

2. Give an example of what you (or someone you know) has tried to do in order to become more of a son or daughter of God.

3. Are you consciously living your life believing that God has already given you everything you need that pertains to "life and godliness"?

4. Why do you think only a fully mature son or daughter can inherit everything the Father has willed to them?

5. Write a personal example of the difference in knowing a truth and experiencing a revelation.

6. Give a personal example of how your true identity is experienced in your true authority.

REINFORCING YOUR IMAGE—PERSONAL REVIEW

True/False

1. Christian growth is the process of becoming who you already are. True_____ False_____

2. Since the Fall, everything in creation struggles with its identity.
True_____ False_____

3. There is no difference between truth and revelation.
True_____ False_____

4. Inherent within your essential identity exists the ability to behave accordingly. True_____ False_____

Multiple Choice

5. According to 1 John 3:1, we
(A) are now the sons of God
(B) will someday be the sons of God

(C) can never become the sons of God

6. In order to inherit everything God has willed for us we must become
   (A) obedient
   (B) sanctified
   (C) fully mature

7. God chastens His sons and daughters because he
   (A) loves us
   (B) is mad at us
   (C) wants to show us who is boss

8. Teachings and beliefs that contradict who the bible says we are in Christ must be
   (A) examined carefully
   (B) cast down (rejected)
   (C) respected

Fill in the Blanks

9. Our spiritual _____ always determines our final _____.

10. Romans 4 tells us that Abraham was first _____ father and then _____ a father because he dared to _____ God.

11. Revelation is actually the truth you and I have _____ and _____.

12. If you do not understand your _____ as a son or daughter of the kingdom, you will live your entire life beneath the _____ of your _____.

STRENGTHENING YOUR IMAGE—KEY BIBLE VERSES

1 John 3:1-2
2 Peter 1:3
I Peter 1:23
Hebrews 12:5-9
Romans 8:14

HIGHLIGHTING YOUR IMAGE—KEY QUOTES

Christian growth is the process of becoming who you already are.

Our identity is a settled fact, but our spiritual maturity is yet to be determined.

You will never discover your true authority until you first discover your true identity.

SHARING YOUR IMAGE—
SUGGESTIONS FOR GROUP DISCUSSION

1. Discuss the ways various religious groups teach how one becomes a son of God.

2. Discuss why only mankind struggles with its identity.

3. Discuss the difference between truth and revelation.

LESSON SEVEN
UNVEILING YOUR ESSENTIAL IDENTITY

Buried beneath the layers of rejection, abandonment, misunderstanding and spiritual ignorance is the person God created you to be. Sometimes the process of unveiling your essential identity is like that of a gold miner blasting through the hard shell of the surface and sifting through tons of crushed stone just to discover that one precious ounce of pure gold.

Many of us have never been taught the skills necessary to "mine the gold" found at the core of our identities. As long as we are blind to our self-worth, we will never discover the priceless qualities that have been deposited deep within our spirits. Unveiling our essential identity is a process, not an event.

This process begins when we understand the power inherent within our self-worth. Our self-worth determines our ability to give and receive love as well as recognize value in those around us. Either consciously or subconsciously, our self-worth sets the agenda for our marriages, careers, personal accomplishment and individual fulfillment in life.

ENEMIES OF YOUR ESSENTIAL IDENTITY

1. Lack of revelation

Ask yourself the question, "Who has the right to define me?" In the presence of insecurity, *someone* or *something* will arise with an agenda to define your life. It may be as general as a self-centered culture or as specific as misguided authority figures, but someone or something will label you. I am convinced that the Word of God, applied through the wisdom of the Holy Spirit, is the only thing that has a right—and is capable—of defining you. But you will never discover your essential identity unless you have eyes to see and ears to hear.

During Jesus' earthly ministry, the Pharisees did not have "ears to hear" His teachings. They listened with a predetermined disposition, considering themselves to be instructors who already knew all they needed. But the disciples were open to the teachings of Jesus. They were eager to learn.

Granted, it is easier to wander aimlessly through life without giving any consideration to whether or not you are living in the reality of your essential identity. It is always easier to assume the identity of another than it is to become yourself.

2. Generational curses

One of the foremost ways that strongholds of insecurity and rejection are established in people's lives is by the spiritual transfer of the sins of the fathers to the children. A child suffering with a distorted self-image is often the product of one or both parents who struggled with the same malaise.

I do not believe this is simply the product of environmental influence. I have ministered to a number of people who were separated from their parents at birth, only to be reunited later in their lives and discover that they were exhibiting the same character traits as their parents.

In his book, *Freedom From Guilt*, Bruce Narramore gives two examples of how strongholds, both positive and negative are passed down generationally. He first traced the descendants of Jonathan Edwards, a fiery American colonial preacher and theologian. Of the 374 descendants tracked, 100 became ministers or missionaries; 100 became professors; 100 were lawyers and judges; 60 were doctors; and 14 were college presidents.

The second man was a convicted criminal named Max Jukes. Of the 917 descendants studied, there were 130 convicted criminals; 310 professional paupers; 400 who were seriously injured or who physically degenerated due to their lifestyles; 60 habitual thieves or pickpockets; and 17 murderers. Only 20 people in this group learned a trade, and 10 of those were taught the trade while in prison.[1]

The unveiling of your essential identity can be hindered because of unresolved issues lurking in the past. Satan operates from the past, while God works from the future. A man will deal with his children exactly as he was dealt with unless he makes a conscious choice to do otherwise. This process will continue generation after generation until the curse is realized and broken through repentance and prayer.

3. Wrong relationships

The most powerful force in the universe, outside of God, is human relationships. Our relationships are the key to our personal success or failure; they will either coach us into destiny or restrict us from our ultimate purpose. Everything that we are today, good and bad, is the product of the people we know and the lessons we've learned.

Wrong relationships are not always comprised of evil people. Many times they are good people trapped in relationships that are simply not right . . . for them. These could include attending a church to which God did not lead you, working in a company that is not conducive to your spiritual health, dating an unbeliever, or being in business with someone who does not honor your value system. Such relationships hold the potential to hinder your spiritual growth and maturity.

Relationships are complex—they have both static and dynamic aspects associated with them. While certain covenant relationships are forever, those people within the relationship are in the process of growing and evolving into who they were created to be.

After seventeen years of marriage, my needs have changed—and so have those of my wife. Thankfully, we committed to a journey, not an event. As we became clearer on who we are individually, we learned to respond positively to each other's growth rather than react in fear.

4. Insecurity

A feeling of insecurity is based upon an inner belief of personal inadequacy. I am convinced that much of the insecurity with which we struggle is not a result of who we are (or who we are not), but rather a result of using a false measuring stick to determine our worth and value. We fall into the trap of comparing ourselves with others and in doing so we block the wisdom of God from revealing our life's purpose. Paul said, in 2 Corinthians 10:12 that those who measure themselves by themselves, and compare themselves among themselves, are not wise.

The danger in comparing ourselves with one another is that we develop the tendency to settle for the lowest common denominator. If I allow my father to become the benchmark for my destiny, then once I have reached his status, I will consider myself as having apprehended the ultimate purpose for my life. In accepting someone else's destiny as the pattern for my life, I have blocked the wisdom of God from revealing my high calling. I have prevented God from revealing my identity. The measuring stick for your destiny is not your husband, wife, brother, sister or classmate; it is the divine pattern established by The Image Maker.

Idealism is the driving force behind insecurity. Instead of accepting the divine design for their lives, people allow society to superimpose an image of the "ideal" man or woman on them.

In his insightful work, *The Search for Significance*, Robert McGee said, "Basing our self-worth on what we believe others think of us causes us to become addicted to their approval.[2]

5. Rejection

Fear is the guardian of rejection. Wherever you find rejection present, you will find fear inviting, reinforcing and protecting it. Man's greatest fear is that he will not be received, respected and loved.

Most of us fear rejection in some form or another. Even though we often take great care to protect our emotions by telling ourselves that it really doesn't matter, we still fall prey to its devastating effect time and again. We even learn to handle the more extreme forms of rejection. We shrug off the words of an irate driver who thinks we are holding up traffic. But the words of a careless parent or teacher telling us we will never amount to anything can devastate us.

Robert S. McGee wrote that

"Rejection can be a very effective, though destructive, motivation. . . . we can send the message that our targeted individual doesn't meet our standards. We can harness this person's instinctive desire for acceptance until we have changed and adapted his or her behavior to suit our tastes and purposes. This is how rejection enables us to control the actions of another human being."[3]

The percentage of people who use rejection as a tool of manipulation is probably larger than we realize. Unfortunately, some pastors manipulate people with a message that declares, "Obey, and you'll be accepted; disobey, and you'll be rejected!" Usually this message goes far beyond the basic commands of the Bible to include the culture of the church as well. We see the same pressure present wherever conformity is required, from politics to prison. Manipulation always distorts the unveiling of essential identity.

6. Unforgiveness

Unforgiveness is the most destructive force in the universe. When we allow unforgiveness access into our lives, we set in motion a chain of circumstances that often results in emotional, spiritual and relational destruction. Forgiveness is for the sake of the offended as much as it is for the offender.

While many myths surround the issue of forgiveness, we need to understand the following three powerful truths

To the degree that we are willing to forgive others, God will forgive us. It's a frightening fact to discover, but many times our attitudes toward one another predetermine God's attitude toward us. Our willingness to forgive men reveals the faithfulness of God.

Forgiveness does not always mean forgetting. While Jeremiah 31:34 says that God does not remember our sins, this does not mean that He suffers from amnesia. God forgives to the degree that He holds no resentment against us and refuses to condemn us based upon those sins of our past.

There is such a thing as righteous remembering, where we keep a clear picture of the past but temper it with grace and mercy. Redemptive remembering should always motivate us toward a better future, it should not tie us to a crippled past.

Oftentimes offenses continue to fester in relationships because acceptance takes the place of forgiveness. Most of us have learned how to "stuff" our hurt and go on without ever being honest with ourselves and with our pain. To deny emotional pain is to deny God's right to heal you. Until you learn to become honest with yourself, you will never be able to be honest with others.

Several years ago God was dealing with me about a relational challenge that I didn't want to face or deal with. Finally, the Holy Spirit spoke to my heart, "Until you face it, you will never discover the grace to displace it."

A wise man once said, "Forgive me, and you will heal yourself. Tolerate me, and you invite more offense." Accepting people is not a righteous substitute for forgiving them. It is possible to forgive people of their sins without accepting their present actions. There is a world of difference between forgiveness and tolerance. You can forgive someone of anything, but you cannot tolerate everything. The teachings of Jesus require us to forgive the offender seventy times seven for his past transgressions, but they do not require us to remain in abusive situations.

7. Perfectionism

Perfectionism is the fear of failure expressed through an over-compensation to succeed at the expense of personal fulfillment. While many perfectionists often appear to be overachievers, their motivation is usually fueled by a desire to gain acceptance and to overcome a poor self-image.

Sometimes a desire to please parents, spouses, or others results in our becoming someone other than whom we were created to be. Pleasing others can prevent the discovery of the divine design that The Image Maker has established for our lives.

DISCOVERING THE DIVINE PERSPECTIVE

Destiny always begins internally and eventually manifests itself externally. That's why you can put a purposeful man in an oppressive environment, and given enough time, he will change it. But conversely, you can put a slothful man in an environment rife with potential, and he will never rise to greatness. Destiny is the result of understanding our essential identity, coming to terms with our security in the will of God and tapping into the passion for the journey.

Abraham changed the course of history because of an internal picture that was formed in his soul when he encountered The Image Maker on the backside of the desert. Moses brought deliverance to his generation because of an internal perspective that was formed when he encountered the great "I AM" in a burning bush. Joseph ruled a nation because of an internal perspective that was formed when he saw his potential in a dream. David served his generation because of an internal perspective of victory that was formed while tending his father's sheep. In each of these men, destiny began with the development of an inner image of victory.

DEVELOPING THE INNER IMAGE

The problem with most of us is that we have never worked long enough on establishing an inner image of victory deep in our soul (mind, will and emotions). We spend most of our time thinking about what we cannot accomplish in life, for whatever reason we believe that we cannot achieve it. "Oh, I could never see myself doing that," we say. "I could never see myself having that." "I don't have enough education or experience. I'll never reach my dreams; I'll never succeed."

Rather than using the creative power of the redeemed spirit to chart a course of victory, many people use it to reinforce a lifestyle of defeat. Through spiritual ignorance, they curse the very thing God has chosen to prosper them in.

Do you want to break free from your pointless existence? Do you really want to transform your life from hopelessness and despair to purpose and productivity? Then you must begin renewing your mind by the Word of God to the pathway He has chosen for your life. And as you do, The Image Maker will unveil your essential identity.

> Do not be conformed to this world, but be transformed by the renewing of your mind, that you may prove what is that good and acceptable and perfect will of God.
> *—Romans 12:2*

DISCOVERING YOUR IMAGE

Several principles incorporated in this lesson are listed below. In your own words, write a brief summary of each principle as you understand it. Or if you choose, you may copy one or two statements from the book.

1. Buried beneath the layers of rejection, abandonment, misunderstanding and spiritual ignorance is the person God created you to be.

2. In the presence of insecurity, *someone* or *something* will arise with an agenda to define your life.

3. One of the foremost ways that strongholds of insecurity and rejection are established in people's lives is by the spiritual transfer of the sins of the fathers to the children.

4. The most powerful force in the universe, outside of God, is human relationships.

5. A feeling of insecurity is based upon an inner belief of personal inadequacy.

6. Fear is the guardian of rejection. Wherever you find rejection present, you will find fear inviting, reinforcing and protecting it.

7. Unforgiveness is the most destructive force in the universe.

8. Perfectionism is the fear of failure expressed through an overcompensation to succeed at the expense of personal fulfillment.

9. Destiny always begins internally and eventually manifests itself externally.

FORMING YOUR IMAGE

The following principles are presented in a format that focuses on personal application. In the space provided after each, write what seems applicable to you.

1. Who, or what, have you allowed to define you? Explain.

2. Do you recognize harmful patterns of behavior in your life that were also present in a parent or other authority figure? If your answer is yes, be specific—name the behavior.

3. Honestly examine your relationships . . . do you think you are involved in relationships detrimental to your spiritual growth and maturity?

4. Do you compare or measure your life to that of others and feel insecure? Explain.

5. Can you think of an ongoing situation in which you feel rejected? If yes, what can you do to change this?

6. Do you harbor unforgiveness toward anyone? If you do, write that person's name here and ask God to help you to forgive.

7. Are you trying to gain acceptance and overcome a poor self-image by trying to please others? If yes, do you now see how this prevents the discovery of God's divine design for your life?

8. Has God given you a dream, a vision, or a strong sense of purpose in a specific area? Write it here and make a renewed commitment to develop that inner image.

REINFORCING YOUR IMAGE—PERSONAL REVIEW

True/False

1. It is always easier to assume the identity of another than it is to become yourself. True_____ False_____

2. Wrong relationships always involve evil people. True_____ False_____

3. If I cannot forget a wrong committed against me, I have not really forgiven that person. True_____ False_____

4. Accepting people is not a righteous substitute for forgiveness. True_____ False_____

Multiple Choice

5. The most powerful force in the universe, outside of God, is
   (A) money
   (B) human relationships
   (C) education

6. Paul said in 2 Corinthians 10:12 that those who compare and measure themselves to others are
   (A) not wise
   (B) intelligent
   (C) seeking reality

7. The most destructive force in the universe is
   (A) crime
   (B) hatred
   (C) unforgiveness

8. Constantly trying to please others can
   (A) make life easier
   (B) keep us out of trouble
   (C) prevent the discovery of God's divine design for your lives

Fill in the Blanks

9. In the presence of insecurity, _____ or
_____ will arise with an agenda to define your
life.

10. The unveiling of your essential identity can be hindered
because of _____ _____
_____ in your _____. Satan works
from the _____, while God works from the
_____.

11. Redemptive remembering should always motivate us toward a
_____ _____, it
should not tie us to a _____
_____.

12. Destiny always begins _____ and eventually manifests itself _____.

STRENGTHENING YOUR IMAGE—KEY BIBLE VERSES

In the space below write the key Bible verses from this lesson. You
might also want to memorize them.

2 Corinthians 10:12
Jeremiah 31:34
Romans 12:2

HIGHLIGHTING YOUR IMAGE—KEY QUOTES

Unveiling our essential identity is a process, not an event.

Satan operates from the past, God works from the future.

Your relationships are the key to your personal success or failure.

Fear is the guardian of rejection.

Unforgiveness is the most destructive force in the universe.

SHARING YOUR IMAGE—
SUGGESTIONS FOR GROUP DISCUSSION

1. Encourage group members to share how the enemies of essential identity (i.e., lack of revelation, wrong relationships, unforgiveness) have prevented them from realizing their self-worth.

2. Share with one another the "dream, vision, or purpose" you feel God has revealed as part of your destiny.

LESSON EIGHT
THE TECHNOLOGY OF THE NEW CREATION

The New Testament epistles reveal a spiritual technology concerning the identity of the new creation. In essence, *technology* in any area or field is "an action (or series of actions) that produces a specific result when applied." The term *spiritual technology* could also be referred to as a "spiritual law," or a "biblical principle." Thus, Redemption is a spiritual technology—a spiritual action that produces a specific result when applied.

The technology of Redemption is not a "hit-or-miss" proposition. This spiritual force is not selectively distributed throughout the world, only finding application in the lives of an elite minority. It is a global operation—freely crossing national boundaries, racial barriers and class distinctions. Consistent with the nature of spiritual law, Redemption is a universally established principle, producing the same result in the life of every person who believes and receives.

God performed in Christ what He wanted to accomplish in every man—in every generation. God boldly asserted all that He had in Christ and then, by virtue of the Holy Spirit, supernaturally joined us to Him. Colossians 1:18 says, "He is the head of the body, the church, who is the beginning, the firstborn from the dead, that in all things He may have the preeminence." The word *beginning* means "the first person in a series, leader." The word denotes not merely the first in a series, but also the source to which the series can be traced. The word *firstborn* implies that because He is the first born, others will follow.

A LIMITED VIEW PRODUCES A INCOMPLETE ATONEMENT

In order to break free from the bondage of a defeated self-image, we must reexamine the commonly accepted views of the church and recover the apostolic technology of the new creation. A twenty-first-century view of these truths, however, affords us both advantages and disadvantages. We have the advantage of seeing the influence of the gospel and how it has changed the course of history. But we also have the disadvantage of viewing New Testament truth through the mosaic of religious interpretation, trying to determine which image is the real one.

Through this apostolic technology, the image of God in man, which was marred in the Fall, is being progressively revealed and restored.

This implies that through this process, man's perverted view of self-image is being clarified and healed. This renewal of our self-image takes place in two specific areas.

First, when the Holy Spirit regenerates us, He also empowers us to resist arrogance and pride, the first perversions of the self-image. In place of those self-destructive elements, He leaves a deposit of thankfulness and humility. We often hear, "I'm just a sinner saved by grace." Although it may sound as if it comes from a posture of humility, those who subscribe to this quality of life lack foundational revelation. The whole purpose of being saved by grace is to remove you from your identity as a sinner. To adopt the position of being "a sinner saved by grace" erodes the apostolic image of all things being new in Christ.

The "once a sinner, always a sinner" view has been offset by the "I have a personal sovereignty" philosophy at the opposite end of the spectrum. Either position is a distortion of the truth. The truth of the matter can only be determined through New Testament revelation in stark contrast to certain aspects of Protestant Reformation that teach a weak doctrine of "limited atonement."

Many of these doctrines, in their most extreme applications, distort the issue of man's worthiness even to be saved. Others, though they may acknowledge Jesus Christ as the initiator of reconciliation, emphasize the work of man as the source of *securing* his own salvation through his good works, apart from grace.

The apostolic technology also speaks to the second type of perversion we have seen—namely an extremely low self-image. Many sincere Christians are more focused on their own personal weakness rather than on their newly developed image as the new creation. It takes an awareness of where you came from contrasted with the revelation of who you now are to maintain spiritual balance in your life.

THE APOSTOLIC CONCEPT OF THE IMAGE OF GOD

A careful study of Paul's writings reveals a "system of truth" that consistently defines his view of the image of God—(1) lost by man, (2) regained by Christ and (3) restored in the new creation. This term, *system of truth*, was first coined by Richard Weymouth in his New Testament translation of Romans 6:17: "But thanks be unto God that you were once in thralldom to sin, but you have now yielded a hearty obedience to that *system of truth* in which you have been instructed" (emphasis added).

This system of truth reveals the technology of Redemption as it relates to the vicarious suffering, substitutionary death and glorious resurrection of Jesus Christ with the restoration of man as the central object of this action.

The death, burial and resurrection of Jesus Christ are the core of the gospel. The same power that God released in the *event* is in the *message*. The gospel perpetuates the same resurrection power that God released in Christ when He raised Him from the dead. All other issues bearing on the abundant life flows from this "core value" that serves as the legal basis for our redemption, regeneration and continual deliverance. (See 1 Peter 1:18-19.)

The clearest definition of *redemption* means "to buy back; to get back; to recover; to ransom; to pay off." God paid the ultimate price for our redemption—the death of His beloved Son. "For as by one man's disobedience many were made sinners, so also by one Man's obedience many will be made righteous" (Romans 5:19). Our redemption includes restoration of everything that was lost in the Fall.

The Genesis account tells us what the curse consists of:

- Man driven from God's presence and banned from eternal life.
- Enmity released between the deceiver and humanity,

resulting in spiritual warfare.
- Unity of the marriage covenant placed under stress—relational disharmony.
- Parental connection placed in jeopardy—pain associated with birthing and rearing children.
- Earth cursed, resulting in drought, famine, pestilence, unstable weather patterns and geological upheaval.
- Man's toil reduced to futility, striving to make a living—he left his position of abundance.
- Death entered the world—physically and spiritually.

The long-term effect of the curse, which came upon everything placed under Adam's dominion, was the gradual distortion of the divine imprint on man.

In one supernatural moment, Redemption removes us out from under the curse and aligns us with the blessing of heaven. We no longer *are* who we once *were*. The apostolic technology reveals Redemption as a "past tense" experience.

> Christ has [past tense] redeemed us from the curse of the law. —Galatians 3:13
> The Father . . .has [past tense] qualified us to be partakers of the inheritance of the saints. —Colossians 1:12
> He [the Father] has [past tense] delivered us from the power of darkness and conveyed us into the kingdom of the Son of His love. —Colossians 1:13
> Who [the Father] has [past tense] blessed us with every spiritual blessing in the heavenly places in Christ. —Ephesians 1:3
> His divine power has [past tense] given to us all things that pertain to life and godliness. —2 Peter 1:3

THE APOSTOLIC IMAGE OF THE CHURCH

Our true identity is what God's Word says about us. The apostolic technology provides us with a detailed description of our new identification. These are a few of our character qualities:

- *Members of Christ's body*—with individual expressions of the nature and character of Jesus (Ephesians 5:30).

- *The sons of God*—sharing in all of Christ's character (1 John 3:1).
- *Zion, the beloved city of God*—a city of refuge in the midst of an environment hostile to our identity (Psalms 125:1).
- *Citizens of the heavenly Jerusalem*—ambassadors of God's kingdom (Ephesians 2:6; 6:20).
- *One new man*—symbolizing our unity with Christ (Ephesians 2:15).
- *Bride of Christ*—chosen to be pure and undefiled (Revelation 21:2).
- *Heirs and joint heirs with Christ*—we share in Christ's inheritance (Romans 8:17).
- *Soldiers in the army of the Lord*—with the right to exercise His authority in the world (2 Timothy 2:3-4).

The new creation is so unique and diverse that it takes dozens of descriptive phrases throughout the Bible to identify who we are in Christ. Even then our individual identities are as diverse as our respective personalities.

IDENTIFICATION BRINGS JUSTIFICATION

By identifying with Adam, we qualify to identify with Christ. By identifying with Christ, we discover the truth about ourselves.

> For you died, and your life is hidden with Christ in God. When Christ who is our life appears, then you also will appear with Him in glory.
>
> —*Colossians 3:3-4*

Identifying with Christ as the Son of Man qualifies us to receive His sacrificial atonement for our fallen nature. It also qualifies us to receive the favored inheritance the Father promised the Son and all who would believe on Him.

> Therefore we were buried with Him through baptism into death, that just as Christ was raised from the dead by the glory of the Father, even so we also should walk in newness of life. For if we have been united together in the likeness of His death, certainly we also shall be in the likeness of His resurrection.
>
> —*Romans 6:4-5*

The technology of Redemption produces the same result in every man who is born of the Spirit of God. As a result of the vicarious suffering, substitutionary death and glorious resurrection of Jesus Christ, you are now redeemed, reconciled and restored. As the new creation, there is no trace left of the person you used to be in your inner man. All things have been made new through the power of His grace.

DISCOVERING YOUR IMAGE

Several principles incorporated in this lesson are listed below. In your own words, write a brief summary of each principle as you understand it. Or if you choose, you may copy one or two statements from the book.

1. Redemption is a spiritual technology—a spiritual action that produces a specific result when applied.

2. In order to break free from the bondage of a defeated self-image, we must reexamine the commonly accepted views of the church and recover the apostolic technology of the new creation.

3. To adopt the position of being "a sinner saved by grace" erodes the apostolic image of all things being new in Christ.

4. A careful study of Paul's writings reveals a "system of truth" that consistently defines his view of the image of God—(1) lost by man, (2) regained by Christ and (3) restored in the new creation.

5. In one supernatural moment, Redemption removes us out from under the curse and aligns us with the blessing of heaven.

6. Our true identity is what God's Word says about us.

FORMING YOUR IMAGE

The following principles are presented in a format that focuses on personal application. In the space provided after each, write what seems applicable to you.

1. Describe the personal results in your life of the spiritual technology of Redemption.

2. Have you ever referred to yourself as a "sinner saved by

grace"? If your answer is yes, why did you do that? Why is this statement in error?

3. Choose an example from the list of curses from the Genesis account and tell how it has affected you.

4. Personalize two of the verses that are used to illustrate the [past tense] of Redemption.

5. Consider the statement, "Our true identity is what God's Word says about us." Then write a description of who you are.

6. What new truth have you discovered about yourself in this lesson?

REINFORCING YOUR IMAGE—PERSONAL REVIEW

True/False

1. The term "spiritual technology" could also be referred to as a spiritual law. True____ False____

2. For a Christian to say, "I'm just a sinner saved by grace," is a correct statement. True____ False____

3. The long-term effect of the cruse was the gradual distortion of the divine imprint on man. True____ False____

4. The technology of Redemption produces different results in believers, depending on how sincere they are. True____ False____

Multiple Choice

5. Our redemption includes the restoration of
(A) only spiritual things
(B) all spiritual things and some physical things
(C) everything lost in the fall

6. The clearest definition of redemption means
   (A) to buy back
   (B) to earn back
   (C) a gift

7. Our true identity is
   (A) what are parents say we are
   (B) what God's Word says we are
   (C) what society says we are

8. The apostolic technology reveals Redemption as
   (A) a past tense experience
   (B) an ongoing experience
   (C) an "on-and-off" experience

Fill in the Blanks

9. God performed in Christ what He wanted to accomplish in
   _____ _____—in _____
   _____.

10. A careful study of Paul's writings reveals a _____
    _____ that consistently defines
    his view of the _____ of _____.

11. The death, burial and resurrection of Jesus Christ are the
    _____ of the _____.

12. By identifying with Adam, we _____ to
    _____ with _____. By identify-
    ing with Christ, we discover the _____ about
    ourselves.

STRENGTHENING YOUR IMAGE—KEY BIBLE VERSES

In the space below write the key Bible verses from this lesson. You might also want to memorize them.

Colossians 1:18
Romans 6:17
Romans 5:19
Galatians 3:13
Colossians 1:13
2 Peter 1:3
Colossians 3:3-4
Romans 6:4-5

HIGHLIGHTING YOUR IMAGE—KEY QUOTES

God performed in Christ what He wanted to accomplish in every man.

The same power that God released in the *event* is in the *message*.

The apostolic technology reveals Redemption as a past tense experience.

Our true identity is what God's Word says about us.

SHARING YOUR IMAGE— SUGGESTIONS FOR GROUP DISCUSSION

1. Group members mention (with one person writing them down) any teachings or ideas that present a "incomplete atonement." Then discuss how these have affected you personally—or someone you know.

2. Using the list of results of the curse, share personal examples of these.

3. From the list of character qualities that describe our new iden-

tification, discuss how you can help one another to walk in these truths.

PART III:
DETERMINING YOUR MISSION

LESSON NINE
LIVING FREE FROM SIN CONSCIOUSNESS

As powerful and undeniable as the Scriptures make freedom from sin consciousness known, some still tend to think that the more conscious we are of sin, the less likely we are to commit acts of sin. But that perspective usually draws us toward increased sinfulness. Why? Because we will always move in the direction of our most dominant thought. That's why Proverbs 23:7 declares, "For as he thinks in his heart, so is he." Our meditation has the power to determine our destination.

Sin consciousness always results in increased sinfulness. However, when we focus on righteousness, we leave little room for the works of iniquity to find a place in our lives. Our personal righteousness in Christ is our most powerful weapon against the attacks of the enemy. Righteousness is both a noun and a verb. It is *who we are* in conjunction with *what we are empowered to do* though the grace of God.

E. W. Kenyon wrote, "The desire to get rid of sin consciousness has given birth to all of the major religions of the world. Few theologians have recognized the fact that sin consciousness is the parent of practically all human religions."[1]

Most people do not realize that religion is man's attempt to gain divine favor based upon *man's terms* rather than upon *God's terms*. At the root of all religion is man's search for significance. *Religion* is *man's acceptance* of God, but *Christianity* is *God's acceptance* of man. Only one person in the universe is qualified to accept you as you are—Jesus Christ.

The writer of Hebrews reveals how God carefully communicated

His word of righteousness throughout the history of man, but has now and forever chosen to reveal its final expression through His Son, Christ Jesus. (See Hebrews 1:1-2.) When we see Jesus, we see the sum total of perfect righteousness, the same measure that is offered to all those who receive His provision.

SEEING BUT NOT PERCEIVING

Beginning with the entrance of original sin into the world, the spirit of condemnation began working to alienate man from the presence of The Image Maker. In every generation following, it has capitalized upon man's propensity toward sin consciousness, thereby blinding him to the opportunity to be accepted by God. Living in a world of darkness, we accepted the lie that we were unworthy to enter the throne room, and we settled for our spiritual displacement. So, what is the solution for our self-imposed exile from the presence of God? We must train ourselves to perceive and believe what the Word of God has to say about our essential identity as the new creation.

In his remarkable book *An Anthropologist on Mars*, Dr. Oliver Sacks tells the story of Virgil, a man who had become blind as a child, yet regained his complete vision in midlife by way of a medical miracle. When the bandages were removed, Virgil could see but had no idea what he was seeing. His first violent visual encounter revealed a blur of light, movement and color—all meaningless. Then out of the blur came the voice of the surgeon, and Virgil realized that this chaos of light and shadow was a face.

Further testing revealed that while Virgil could see images of people, light and color—even his own reflection—he remained "mentally blinded." He had no way of interpreting what he saw; his cerebral capabilities had never been trained for a day like this. In order to comprehend his visual surroundings, Virgil's mind had to be trained to perceive his visual surroundings. He experienced what we Christians would call, in a spiritual sense, the renewing of his mind. The process was gradual, painful and at times halted, but Virgil finally began to connect with his "sighted" world. It was only when Virgil moved beyond *seeing* and moved into *perception* that he could begin to appreciate the beauty and significance of the world around him.[2]

This medical miracle is similar to the story in the Gospel of Mark of the blind man. When Jesus touched his eyes *initially*, the blind man said he could "see men like trees, walking" (Mark 8:24). The next verse says, "Then He [Jesus] put His hands on his eyes *again* and made him look up. And he was restored and saw everyone clearly." The first touch restored the man's *vision*, but a second touch was needed to restore his *perception*.

This describes the spiritual condition of many Christians. Out of the slumber of sin consciousness, we were awakened to the infinite glory of our salvation, and yet we "see men like trees, walking." We have sight, but no comprehension; we have vision, but no perception. We have seen the beauty of our salvation, but we must press on to break free from the mental blindness that holds us captive to a limited experience.

It is high time for our generation to recover an understanding of what it means to live as the sons of God, free from shame and the destructive effects of sin consciousness. Paul put it like this, "Awake to righteousness, and do not sin" (1 Corinthians 15:34). The world is waiting for the awakening of those who have been made the righteousness of God in Christ.

Through the Spirit, Christ offered himself as an unblemished sacrifice, freeing us from all those dead-end efforts to make ourselves respectable, so that we can live all out for God.—Hebrews 9:13, The Message

PRACTICE MAKES PERMANENT

We have heard it said, "Practice makes perfect." But that is not altogether true. In reality, practice makes permanent—whether right or wrong. As a tournament archer, I spent weeks practicing only to discover that while I built up strength, my form was all wrong. The long hours of practice made my bad form permanent, not perfect. Correcting the problem was a matter of going back to the basics and reprogramming my mind to the information needed to adjust my form.

Struggling with sin consciousness has become a permanent way of life for many Christians because they have not had a revelation of what it means to live righteous consciously. Practicing condemnation, either on ourselves or on those around us, gives a permanent foothold to this spiritually debilitating force. Condemnation aborts spiritual confidence and destroys spiritual security.

For if our heart condemns us, God is greater than our heart, and knows all things. Beloved, if our heart does not condemn us, we have confidence toward God.—1 John 2:20-21

Did you perceive that? God is greater than your self-imposed condemnation! His grace is infinitely greater than your personal weakness.

At the root of all condemnation is a lie that says, "You're not worthy enough . . . God doesn't really accept you . . . You will never become who you should be." Condemnation drowns out the voice of confidence. Condemnation reduces us to crawling tentatively into the presence of God as intruders rather than entering boldly as sons in whom the Father is well pleased!

One of the most forceful chapters in the New Testament relating to being liberated from sin consciousness is Hebrews 10.

> For the law, having a *shadow* of the good things to come, and not the *very image* of the things, can never with these same sacrifices, which they offer continually year by year, make those who approach perfect. For then would they not have ceased to be offered? For the worshipers, once purified, would have no more *consciousness of sins*. But in those sacrifices there is a *reminder* of sins every year.
>
> —*Hebrews 10:1-3,* emphasis added

This writer by revelation goes on to clearly define the difference between shadow and substance. In verse 10, he announces, "By that [His] will we have been sanctified through the offering of the body of Jesus Christ once for all." Verse 14 states, "For by **one offering** He has **perfected forever** those who are being sanctified."

Hebrews chapter 10 uses the phrases "once *purified*," "have been *sanctified*," "hearts *sprinkled*," and "bodies *washed*." These words are what the Greek language calls the perfect tense. This tense conveys a "completed action that has lingering effects or that leaves an ongoing result or condition." For example, the cry of Jesus from the cross, "It is finished!" (John 19:30), is in the perfect tense, showing us that the *results* and *effects* of His sacrificial death are anything but over and finished.

When we accepted Christ, we accepted *freedom* from sin con-sciousness—a freedom that continues to have a personal application in my life and yours. This freedom is greater than my personal abil-ity to keep the law—it is a power that will not surrender under the crushing shame of personal failure.

Now watch this principle: If I choose the Law, which was but a shadow, I will remain with a constant reminder of my sin and never break free from a consciousness of it. However, if I choose the sub-stance—Christ and His forever settled work of righteousness—I will come out of the poverty of sin consciousness and move into the wealth of a "rightness with God" mind-set!

As I mentioned in a previous lesson, I believe that the church has majored on behavior modification instead of focusing on identity revelation. The real problem with behavior modification is that it may leave you with a change of conduct, but it is powerless to impart righteousness, peace and joy. When you fully awaken to righteousness and begin to live in the reality of who you were made to be in Christ Jesus, temptation cannot destroy you, personal fail-ure cannot abort your purpose, and condemnation can no longer hold you captive. Your identity as a son of the Highest authorizes you to live in this world, even as He lived in this world. Open your eyes to the wonder of who you are! As you live and move and have your being in Christ, you are forever secure in your position as a son of righteousness.

SEEING THE PROBLEM, PRESCRIBING THE CURE

To conclude this study on living free from sin consciousness, let's take a look at the poisonous effects of sin consciousness, along with the spiritual antidote. The effects of sin consciousness are as follows:

Condemnation	Depression
Guilt	Shame
Unworthiness	Torment
Insecurity	Self-rejection
Weak faith	

Struggling to feel accepted by God and others.

Lacking the freedom and boldness to enter the Father's presence.

The solution to sin consciousness is found in renewing your mind with the following principles from the Word of God:

> I have been created in the image of God (Genesis 1:26).
> I have been regenerated into the likeness of God (John 3:6).
> I have confidence that God loves and accepts me (Ephesians 1:6).
> As a son of God, I am pure from the defilement of the world (1 John 3:3).
> When I fail, God will not abandon me (Hebrews 13:5).
> As I walk in the Spirit, I am free from condemnation (Romans 8:1).
> As I love God and others, I increase my capacity to feel loved (1 John 4:12).
> As I love God and others, I am free from fear (1 John 4:18).
> As His child, I am always welcome in the presence of God (Hebrews 10:19).

My personal worth is based upon the price Jesus paid for my Redemption, not upon my personal ability to perform correctly every time I am confronted with temptation.

God has a plan for my life that involves the fulfillment of my personal destiny.

Even though I have faults and failures, I want to change. God is working to change me one step at a time. Furthermore, while I am in the process of changing, I can still enjoy life.

Because I am accepted of God, I can accept others. As I sow seeds of unconditional acceptance, I will reap a harvest of unconditional acceptance.

DISCOVERING YOUR IMAGE

Several principles incorporated in this lesson are listed below. In your own words, write a brief summary of each principle as you understand it. Or if you choose, you may copy one or two statements from the book.

1. As powerful and undeniable as the Scriptures make freedom from sin consciousness known, some still tend to think that the more conscious we are of sin, the less likely we are to commit acts of sin.

2. Beginning with the entrance of original sin into the world, the spirit of condemnation began working to alienate man from the presence of The Image Maker.

3. We have heard it said, "Practice makes perfect." But that is not altogether true. In reality, practice makes permanent—whether right or wrong.

4. When we accepted Christ, we accepted *freedom* from sin consciousness—a freedom that continues to have a personal application in my life and yours.

5. As you live and move and have your being in Christ, you are forever secure in your position as a son of righteousness.

6. The solution to sin consciousness is found in renewing your mind with appropriate principles from the Word of God.

FORMING YOUR IMAGE

The following principles are presented in a format that focuses on personal application. In the space provided after each, write what seems applicable to you.

1. If there are areas of sin to which you are particularly prone (i.e., lying, cheating, drinking too much, extra-marital affairs)

how are you dealing with it? Is it on your mind a lot as you strive to avoid it? Or is your mind more on Christ and His complete provision for your righteousness?

2. Give a personal example (present or past) of how condemnation alienated you from God's presence.

3. Are there any areas of spiritual conduct where you recognize that while the practicing of this conduct has become permanent, it has not produced perfection? Explain.

4. Personalize the statement from Hebrews 10:14, "For by one offering He has perfected forever those who are being sanctified."

5. Using the list of poisonous effects of sin consciousness near the end of the text for this lesson, list the ones that fit you now (or have in the past).

6. From the list of Bible statements at the end of the text, write the ones that would be most helpful to you today.

REINFORCING YOUR IMAGE—PERSONAL REVIEW

True/False

1. We will always move in the direction of our most dominant thought. True____ False____

2. Our most powerful weapon against the attacks of the enemy is self-control. True____ False____

3. Condemnation drowns out the voice of confidence. True____ False____

4. Depression and torment are two of the poisonous effects of sin consciousness. True____ False____

Multiple Choice

5. Sin consciousness always results in
   (A) holiness
   (B) increased sinfulness
   (C) better relationships

6. If I choose the Law . . . I will
   (A) remain with a constant reminder of my sin
   (B) be a moral person
   (C) be free from sin

7. At the root of all condemnation is
   (A) a lie that says, "You're not worthy"
   (B) the truth that you are guilty
   (C) a poor self-image

8. The words "purified, sanctified, sprinkled and washed" in Hebrews, Chapter 10 are
   (A) future tense
   (B) perfect tense
   (C) past tense

Fill in the Blanks

9. We must _____ ourselves to _____ and _____ what the Word of God has to say about our _____ _____ as the new creation.

10. Condemnation aborts _____ _____ and destroys _____ _____.

11. Hebrews 10:14 says that by _____ _____ He has _____ _____ those who are being sanctified.

12. My personal worth is based upon the price _____

paid for my Redemption, not upon my _____
_____ to _____
_____ every time I am confronted with temptation.

STRENGTHENING YOUR IMAGE—KEY BIBLE VERSES

In the space below write the key Bible verses from this lesson. You might also want to memorize them.

Proverbs 23:7
Hebrews 9:13
1 John 2:20-21
Hebrews 10:1-3

HIGHLIGHTING YOUR IMAGE—KEY QUOTES

Sin consciousness always results in increased sinfulness.

At the root of all religion is man's search for significance.

Practice makes permanent.

Condemnation drowns out the voice of confidence.

SHARING YOUR IMAGE—
SUGGESTIONS FOR GROUP DISCUSSION

1. Discuss how various religions (and even various groups within Christianity) use sin consciousness in ways that drive people away from God rather than to Him.

2. Use the two lists at the end of the text of this lesson to help one another recognize the poisonous effects of sin consciousness and the solution for it. You might want to add to the list of scripture statements.

LESSON TEN
INVITING THE INCARNATION

Every righteous father desires to reproduce himself in his sons. This is what The Image Maker accomplished in us through the ongoing incarnation.

The prophet Isaiah revealed the divine intention concerning the Incarnation of the Hope of Israel:

> Therefore the Lord Himself will give you a sign: Behold, the virgin shall conceive and bear a Son, and shall call His name Immanuel.
>
> *—Isaiah 7:14*

The coming Messiah was predestined to be called *Immanuel*, which means "God with us" or, more literally translated, "Incarnation." The word *incarnate* simply means, "to embody in flesh, to put into or represent in concrete, tangible form." The Image Maker bridged the chasm between sinless Deity and sinful humanity through the Incarnation.

Jesus Christ was no less than the mediator between two worlds. As heaven's representative on earth, He revealed the Father "full of grace and truth." As earth's representative in the heavenlies, He revealed the Father's love for fallen man before all creation.

NEW BEGINNING FOR MANKIND

The first chapter of the Gospel of John serves as the New Testament counterpart of the Book of Genesis. It is a spiritual overlay of the Old Testament book of beginnings, therein revealing the pattern for kingdom living. John's opening statement establishes the basis for the Incarnation:

> In the beginning was the Word, and the Word was with God, and the Word was God. . . . and the Word became flesh and dwelt among us.
>
> —*John 1:1, 14*

Jesus was fundamentally different from every child born in Bethlehem on that cool fall evening. This infant contained the spiritual blueprint for the restoration of man and the destruction of man's enemy.

THE IMPRINT OF THE FATHER

The final words God spoke before leaving Israel in four hundred years of silence were these:

> Behold, I will send you Elijah the prophet before the coming of the great and dreadful day of the Lord. And **he will turn the hearts of the fathers to the children, and the hearts of the children to their fathers,** lest I come and strike the earth with a curse.
>
> —*Malachi 4:5-6* (emphasis added)

When John the Baptist broke the silence of heaven ten generations later, he did so in the spirit and power of Elijah, **restoring the connection between the heavenly Father and His wayward sons.** John's ministry prepared the way for man to be reconciled to God and to one another.

The Image Maker's purpose in uniting fathers and sons was in order for the progeny to regain their identity so that they might fulfill their divine destiny. In a sociological, psychological and spiritual sense, it is the imprint of the Father that instills a sense of true identity in the child.

Perhaps you are one who struggles with a lack of worth and value because you were raised in a home with an absentee father. If that is the case, then may this be a word of deliverance for you. You have a Father. You have a heavenly Father who lovingly crafted you, who continually cares for you and will not leave you nor forsake you. You have a loving "Dad" who is more committed to your spiritual development and ultimate purpose than you are.

Every righteous father desires to reproduce himself in his son. I distinctly remember daydreaming as a young father as I anticipated the spiritual, physical and emotional development of my three sons. I longed for the day when they could hunt, fish and climb mountains with me. As our three sons progressed through early childhood development, I saw myself in almost every action they took. Some of those actions were cause for joy; others were cause for personal adjustment and parental correction. For good and bad, I had successfully reproduced myself in my sons.

Someone once said, "Christianity is Christ received, realized and reproduced." The very genius of Christianity is the Father's ability to reproduce Himself in our lives through the implement of His life-producing Word. Through the new birth experience, the Father once again takes humanity into partnership with Himself. The Image Maker is in the process of developing the family business of "Jesus Christ and Sons."

THE ONGOING INCARNATION

As shocking as it may seem to one who has never heard this principle before, the Incarnation did not end with the birth of the only begotten Son of God. The New Testament writers eventually lead us beyond the Incarnation of Christ into the ongoing incarnation of the present-day body of Christ.

The first century church understood this, and their actions resulted in their first being called "Christians" at Antioch. The term *Christian* literally means "little Christs" or "little anointed ones." Even the world recognized that these first-century believers were living their lives in the image and likeness of the Son of God. This is the process of the ongoing Incarnation. Just as the Word became flesh in Bethlehem, the Word continues to become flesh in Antioch. The Word of God, unrestrained, contains the power to reproduce itself over and over and over again.

FULFILLING THE ULTIMATE GOAL

The mission of the church is to be the body of which Christ is the Head. We have been divinely crafted to be the completion of Christ in the same way that a head needs a body in order to complete a person. The church is called to complete the Person of

Christ. While Jesus Christ is not incomplete in His essence or His character, He is incomplete in His ultimate mission. Just as you need your body in order to complete your assignment on earth, so does Jesus Christ!

The analogy of the human body is Paul's favorite description of the church. What is the job of your body? It has one primary purpose—to fulfill the dictates of your head. When your brain says, "Move your arm," you move your arm. If your brain says one thing and your body does another, you have disorder, and you cannot fulfill your purpose. Your body is designed to obey your head. And in a like sense, we are the body that has been lovingly designed and carefully crafted to obey the Head, the Lord Jesus Christ.

With nearly fifty years of history in classical Pentecostalism, Pastor Tommy Reid wrote:

"I believe the greatest revelation of the Holy Spirit to the church today is who we are in Christ. Until we learn that we are the ongoing incarnation, and until we learn our union with Him, and His union with us, we cannot comprehend the truth of Christianity."[1]

Union with Christ is the central theme of the plan of regeneration and the subsequent overcoming life.

We are one with Christ in His crucifixion (Galatians 2:20).

We are one with Him in His resurrection (Galatians 2:20).

We are one with Him in His glorious ascension (Ephesians 2:6).

We are one with Him in His ongoing mission to restore that which was lost by Adam in the Garden of Eden. This is the spiritual reality of the Incarnation.

F. J. Huegel wrote in his classic book *Bone of His Bone*: "The Christian life is a participation, not an imitation."[2]

God is in the process of performing the very same thing in your life as He did in the life of Jesus Christ. Because of your trust in His Son, you have become a necessary agent in the ongoing work of reconciling all things back to the Father. The New Covenant order of reconciliation is, "God . . . in Christ reconciling the world to Himself: (2 Corinthians 5:19).

This is why the apostles could use such revolutionary language when describing the nature of the new creation: "Ye are the body of Christ, and members in particular" (1 Corinthians 12:27, KJV). What a powerful concept! To be joined with the God of glory through the investment of His Word in our lives is not an easy concept to grasp.

This Is a Great Mystery

There are mysteries beyond our grasp that are bound up in the supernatural selection of Mary, the overshadowing of the Holy Spirit and the miraculous conception of Jesus. How can one be fully God and yet fully man? It is incomprehensible how the Son of God operated within the boundaries of human limitation so as to contain His Deity on the pathway to the cross. But this is fact—Bible fact.

When addressing the Ephesians church concerning the wonder of the Incarnation, Paul said:

> And He put all things under His feet, and gave Him to be head over all things to the church, which is His body, the fullness of Him who fills all in all.
>
> —*Ephesians 1:22-23*

The apostle related this spiritual reality to the marriage union in Ephesians 5, and said, "This is a great mystery." The word *mystery* simply means "a secret that can only be known to the initiated." This incarnational principle can only be understood by those who have genuinely experienced it and have come to accept it as God's model for reconciliation in the earth. Yet, many Christians fail to grasp the full significance of this *mystery*.

Becoming One With Christ

When you are born again, your spirit is joined (fused together) with the Lord Jesus Christ, and you become one spirit with Him. This is more than figurative speech or symbolic imagery. This eternal truth is mysteriously supernatural. The church is the "mystical body of Christ." Don't water this principle down! Don't rationalize it away! Read it, believe it and receive it!

Concerning the Incarnation, Frederick Buechner said, "It is untheological. It is unsophisticated. It is undignified. But according to Christianity, it is the way things are."[3] The divine order of the Incarnation is God in Christ, followed by Christ in you, the hope of glory.

SEVEN PRINCIPLES OF INCARNATIONAL LIVING

1. *You are not the same person that you once were.*

After the new birth experience, you are the "new man" striving to overcome rather than the "old man" struggling to reform. The basis of your essential identity has changed—you are a new creature in Christ.

2. *Your future is not the same as it once was.*

Along with a transformation of identification, you also experienced a radical alteration of your destination. The new birth not only redeems your identity, but it also restructures the patterns of life that result in your destiny. Your future has now been reconciled with the plans and purposes that God has for your life.

3. *Even though you are the new creation, you still need the anointing to succeed in life.*

Although Jesus was fully God, as a man He had to rely upon the power of the anointing in order to succeed. (See Acts 10:28.) The *anointing* is the empowering agent that energizes the new creation with the life of heaven. Through the power of the Holy Spirit, we continually experience increasing dimensions of the glory of God in our lives.

4. *Your potential in life is unlimited.*

The purpose of the cross was to defeat the power of the enemy and to reconcile men back to God, thereby removing every fleshly limitation from your life. All things are possible to the new creation that receives the Word of God as the pattern for living. "I can do all things through Christ who strengthens me" (Philippians 4:13).

5. *You must guard your new life in Christ.*

Once you understand who you are and whom you represent, you will become careful with your actions in life. Even those actions that may be "acceptable" for others may not be conducive to your life's purpose.

6. *You are God's representatives to the lost and dying world.*

In 2 Corinthians 5:20, Paul describes the new creation as "ambassadors," pleading with men "for His sake to lay hold of the divine favor [now offered you] and be reconciled to God." Our mission is to reconnect the world to Him. The word *represent* means "to present the same thing once again."

As members of the body of Christ, we are in this world with a mission of representing Jesus to our generation. We are called to be "living epistles, seen and read of all men" (See 2 Corinthians 3:2-3).

7. Do not judge your future by the afflictions of your present.

If you had been an observer in Palestine during the life, death and burial of Jesus Christ, you would have never anticipated His redemptive impact upon the entire world. His own disciples did not anticipate the universal consequence of His personal actions. It was only after the Resurrection that everything became clear to them. Likewise, if you judge the success of your future based on the light affliction of your present struggle, you will miss the exceeding weight of glory that is being formed within you.

Our relationship as the new creation is so secure that Paul could ask the question, "Who can separate me from the love of Christ?", knowing full well the answer in advance. No one. Absolutely no one. You are in the process of becoming who you already are.

DISCOVERING YOUR IMAGE

Several principles incorporated in this lesson are listed below. In your own words, write a brief summary of each principle as you understand it. Or if you choose, you may copy one or two statements from the book.

1. Every righteous father desires to reproduce himself in his sons. This is what The Image Maker accomplished in us through the ongoing incarnation.

2. The Image Maker's purpose in uniting fathers and sons was in order for the progeny to regain their identity so that they might fulfill their divine destiny.

3. The Incarnation did not end with the birth of the only begotten Son of God; it is the ongoing incarnation of the present-day body of Christ.

4. The mission of the church is to be the body of which Christ is the Head.

5. We are one with Him in His ongoing mission to restore that which was lost by Adam in the Garden of Eden.

6. The first two principles of Incarnational living are (1) you are not the same person you once were, (2) your future is not the same as it once was.

FORMING YOUR IMAGE

The following principles are presented in a format that focuses on personal application. In the space provided after each, write what seems applicable to you.

1. Describe in personal terms how God, your Father, is reproduced in you, His child.

2. As the spiritual offspring of God, what do you see as your divine destiny?

3. How is the "Word" made flesh a reality in your life?

4. How would you describe your function in the body of Christ?

5. From personal experience (or from personal expectations) how would you describe your participation with Christ in His ongoing mission to restore that which was lost by Adam in the Garden of Eden?

6. How are you different from what you used to be? How does this affect your future?

REINFORCING YOUR IMAGE—PERSONAL REVIEW

True/False

1. Jesus was fundamentally different from every child born. True_____ False _____

2. The Incarnation refers only to the birth of Jesus. True_____ False_____

3. The analogy of the human body is Paul's favorite description of the church. True_____ False_____

4. The new birth not only redeems your identity, it also restructures the patterns of life that result in your destiny. True_____ False___

Multiple Choice

5. Malachi 4:5-6 speaks of turning the hearts of
   (A) husbands to wives
   (B) different races to one another
   (C) fathers to children and children to fathers

6. Believers were first called Christians at
   (A) Antioch
   (B) Rome
   (C) Jerusalem

7. The word *mystery* means
   (A) something that cannot be known
   (B) a secret that can only be know to the initiated
   (C) something we learn at school

8. Your potential in life is
   (A) unlimited
   (B) uncertain
   (C) limited

Fill in the Blanks

9. The infant Jesus contained the _____ _____ for the _____ of man and the _____ of the enemy.

10. The divine order of the Incarnation is God in _____, followed by Christ in _____, the hope of glory.

11. The anointing is the _____ _____ that energizes the new creation with the _____ of _____.

12. Do not judge your _____ by the afflictions of your _____.

STRENGTHENING YOUR IMAGE—KEY BIBLE VERSES

In the space below write the key Bible verses from this lesson. You might also want to memorize them.

Isaiah 7:14
John 1:1, 14

Malachi 4:5-6
1 Corinthians 12:27
Ephesians 1:22-23
Philippians 4:13

HIGHLIGHTING YOUR IMAGE—KEY QUOTES

Every righteous father desires to reproduce himself in his son.

Christianity is Christ received, realized and reproduced.

The mission of the church is to be the body of which Christ is the head.

You are not the same person you once were.

SHARING YOUR IMAGE—
SUGGESTIONS FOR GROUP DISCUSSION

1. Identify some of the many "members" of the body of Christ represented by your group. Then mention other "members" needed to complete the body of Christ.

2. Use the "Seven Principles of Incarnational Living" as a guide for group discussion.

LESSON ELEVEN
TRANSFORMING YOUR THEOLOGY INTO BIOLOGY

When The Image Maker came to earth in the likeness of human flesh, He revealed the vast difference between divine life and human life. Although He lived as a man, He chose to live according to the value system of heavenly life. Not only was Jesus born from above, but He also drew His life source from above. When He demonstrated the pattern for living, He revealed to us the immense difference between those things birthed of the Spirit and those things birthed of the flesh.

This distinction was so vivid that there was no misunderstanding over the identity of His first-generation followers. They were reviled, persecuted, renounced and rejected, but they were never ignored. The separation between those who professed faith in Christ and those who did not was far more sharply defined than it is today.

I am convinced that those characteristics that distinguished the first-generation church from the unregenerate world were foundational issues rather than superficial ones. They didn't just live differently from the rest of culture—they *were fundamentally* different. They were identified because they evidenced their new personhood with a brand-new lifestyle. They understood their distinction as the body of Christ. They were fully convinced of their essential identity and their ultimate destiny.

These first century believers were in the process of "fleshing out" the Word of God on a daily basis. Their theology was in the process of becoming their biology.

INCARNATION OR INSTITUTION

I believe the real difference between first-century Christianity and Christianity in the twenty-first century is not found in society's attitude toward us; the real difference is found in whom we perceive ourselves to be. In between the Word *incarnate* and the Word that became *institutionalized*, the first-century church existed in great power and glory.

The choice every generation has faced since the first-century church is found in 2 Corinthians 3, and it is this: Will we allow the Word to become *incarnate* or *institutionalized* in our lives? The choice is ours—letter or Spirit, institution or incarnate, epitaph or biography.

BECOMING AN EVERYDAY CHRISTIAN

The Word became flesh and blood, and *moved into the neighborhood.* We saw the glory with our own eyes, the one-of-a-kind glory, like Father, like Son, generous inside and out, true from start to finish.
—*John 1:14, The Message,* emphasis added

The journey toward reconciliation began when the Word became flesh. Before God could redeem fallen humanity, the Incarnation had to become more than a concept. It had to transcend a strategic plan of action; it had to be invested into humanity.

The radical nature of being an "everyday" Christian demands that you present your body a living sacrifice, refusing to be conformed to the spirit of the world, as you renew your mind to the revelation of God's perfect will for your life. In order to pursue the perfect will of God for your life, at some point you will have to expand your operative theology.

I am convinced that the Word of God contains a number of areas of critical concern that are never really addressed because we are afraid of the resulting implications. Deep down we know that if we really believe everything that this Book has to say, then we are going to have to be responsible to live in a way to which we have not yet surrendered. Jesus said, "To whom much is given, from him much will be required" (Luke 12:48). Yet the nature of religion is to settle for far less than we have been offered through the power of the gospel. Karl Barth scathingly indicted the theological community when he said, "The Word became flesh—and then through theologians, it became words again."[1]

As we grow in Christ, we tend to develop this internal navigational tool that carefully directs us around the hot spots in the Word of God in order to preserve self. The problem with self-preservation is that you cannot preserve the image of self and that of Christ at the same time.

IDENTIFY TO RECONCILE

Therefore, if anyone is in Christ, he is a new creation; . . . [God] has reconciled us to Himself through Jesus Christ, and has given us the ministry of reconciliation . . . and has committed to us the word of reconciliation.
—*2 Corinthians 5:17-19*

The chronological order in which Paul speaks is critical to a full understanding of our mission in life. We have been given the "ministry" of reconciliation—even before we were given the "word" of reconciliation.

These two words contain the key to our involvement in the ministry of reconciliation. The Greek word for "ministry" is *diakonia* from which we derive the word *deacon*, better defined as a "servant or attendant." The Greek word *logos*, translated "word," literally means the "divine expression" or "the spoken word including the thought."

Paul says that following the *diakonia* of reconciliation, we have been given the *logos* of reconciliation. In other words, we are the "servants" of reconciliation long before we are the "announcers" of reconciliation. We cannot reconcile what we have not served. The very nature of the word *reconciliation* denotes personal involvement.

Jesus had to make contact with the woman at the well in order to reconcile her. He had to make contact with the thief on the cross in order to redeem him.

Consider the position of a hostage negotiator. In order to reconcile the hostage with freedom, he will have to place himself in a position that may not be comfortable to him—even a place of grave danger or personal risk. If necessary, he will place himself in an environment that isn't altogether friendly with his belief system.

That's what Jesus did when the woman at the well said to Him, "Don't you realize that you're a Jew and I'm a Samaritan, and this environment is hostile toward your identity?"

When Jesus walked the seashore of Galilee healing the broken-hearted and setting free the captive, He compassionately identified with the broken and the outcast. Yet He did not enter into the common experience that led them into their state of brokenness. He did not relate to them on the lowest common denominator.

True intercession is always born out of identification, which is not always common experience. Sometimes we confuse the two and end up with the warped perspective that we have to experience what others have experienced in order to effectively relate to them. Wrong! There is a difference between spiritual identification and common experience.

In other words, if you've messed up your life by committing adultery, I don't have to commit adultery in order to identify with the pain of what you are going through. We don't identify based upon a common experience; we identify based upon my compassionate concern for you. Galatians 6:1 speaks of where our greatest identification should lie.

Brethren, if a man is overtaken in any trespass, you who are spiritual restore such a one in a spirit of gentleness, considering yourself lest you also be tempted.

Your greatest identification should lie in being a son of God. From that operational base of purity and power, you are enabled to reconcile others.

Identification is more than mere human sympathy; it is compassionate interaction. God has called us to *empathize* with the world, not to *sympathize* with the world.

The first key to effectively reaching this generation is found in compassionately identifying with suffering humanity while at the same time not allowing ourselves to be overcome by the very things that are destroying them. Identification does not mean participation in the very thing that is destroying another.

BE A CONTAGIOUS CHRISTIAN

The second key to developing the ministry of reconciliation is to become a contagious Christian. If we do not demonstrate a quality of life greater than that which the world already experiences, where is the incentive for change? If our lives do not reflect the answers that Christ offers to the questions of secular man, then what are we really saying to society?

Some people have difficulty in evangelism because they don't really believe in the product. It's difficult to "sell" what you don't believe in, because your life presentation lacks passion. Society is attracted to passionate people. Passionate people are contagious.

Most people find it easy to pursue their real passion in life when they discover what comes naturally to them and what they find fulfilling. What motivates certain people to enter politics, law, medicine, aeronautics, quantum physics, computer programming or athletics? The driving force is passion. Passionate people are persuasive; they are contagious, and they are effective.

DEMONSTRATING THE MESSAGE

The real challenge we encounter in this postmodern culture is to make Christ attractive to all men. And the way we do that is by simply allowing Him to shine forth the beauty of His resurrected life through us. Jesus said, "If you'll lift Me up, I'll do the real work here." (See John 12:32.) Our responsibility is to present the person of Christ with passion and compassion, and He will draw men near.

As much as the unbelieving world would like to understand the true identity of the church, they cannot, for they are spiritually blind. The unregenerate man is incapable of understanding the theology of incarnation, which only leaves him with the picture of our demonstration. They have taken the same position as many others in first-century Palestine who refused to acknowledge Jesus as the Messiah and yet were drawn to Him because of His miracles. They did not understand how He could be God in the flesh, but they were attracted to His character qualitites as a peacemaker and a champion of the downtrodden, the hurting and the outcast.

Even though the world may not understand your theological identity as a son of God, they will know you by your fruit. And when they see your good works, they will glorify your Father in heaven (Matthew 5:16). When you let the light of honesty and integrity shine to your friends in corporate America, then you have given them an invitation to glorify the Father. When you raise sons and daughters who love God and serve the kingdom, then you have given your neighborhood an invitation to glorify the Father in heaven. When you let the light of a joyful, peaceful home shine to your lost family members, you have given them an invitation to glorify the Father. Even if they don't understand your identity, they will at least consider your demonstration.

DISCOVERING YOUR IMAGE

Several principles incorporated in this lesson are listed below. In your own words, write a brief summary of each principle as you understand it. Or if you choose, you may copy one or two statements from the book.

1. When The Image Maker came to earth in the likeness of human flesh, He revealed the vast difference between divine life and human life.

2. The real difference between first-century Christianity and Christianity in the twenty-first century is not found in society's attitude toward us, but in whom we perceive ourselves to be.

3. The radical nature of being an "everyday" Christian demands that you present your body a living sacrifice, refusing to be conformed to the spirit of the world, as you renew your mind to the revelation of God's perfect will for your life.

4. We have been given the "ministry" of reconciliation—even before we were given the "word" of reconciliation.

5. True intercession is always born out of identification, which is not always common experience.

6. The second key to developing the ministry of reconciliation is to become a contagious Christian.

FORMING YOUR IMAGE

The following principles are presented in a format that focuses on personal application. In the space provided after each, write what seems applicable to you.

1. From your personal perspective, give one or two examples of the difference between that which is birthed of the Spirit and that which is birthed of the flesh.

2. How do you perceive yourself as a Christian?

3. Give a personal example of how you can present your body a living sacrifice.

4. Give an example (personal if possible) of the "ministry" of reconciliation at work.

5. Share a personal experience of helping and encouraging someone who was in a situation you had never experienced.

6. Do you consider yourself to be a "contagious" Christian. Explain.

REINFORCING YOUR IMAGE—PERSONAL REVIEW

True/False

1. In the First-century church, the separation between those who professed faith in Christ and those who did not was not as sharply defined as today. True____ False____

2. You cannot preserve the image of self and the image of Christ at the same time. True____ False____

3. True intercession is always born out of common experience. True____ False____

4. The world may not understand your theological identity as a son of God, but they will know you by your fruit. True____ False____

Multiple Choice

5. The real difference between First-century Christianity and Christianity today is
   (A) society's attitude toward us
   (B) separation of church and state

(C) whom we perceive ourselves to be

6. The very nature of the word *reconciliation* denotes
   (A) a law suit
   (B) personal involvement
   (C) church membership

7. The Greek word for ministry" is best defined as
   (A) servant or attendant
   (B) spiritual leadership
   (C) equality

8. Passionate people are
   (A) emotionally unstable
   (B) persuasive and effective
   (C) lacking self-control

Fill in the Blanks

9. In between the Word _____ and the Word
   that became _____, the first-century
   church existed in great power and glory.

10. Karl Barth said, "The Word became _____—and then
    through theologians, it became _____ again.

11. Identification is more than human _____; it
    is compassionate _____.

12. We make Christ attractive to all men by _____
    Him to _____ _____ the beauty of
    His _____ life through _____.

STRENGTHENING YOUR IMAGE—KEY BIBLE VERSES

In the space below write the key Bible verses from this lesson. You
might also want to memorize them.

John 1:14
2 Corinthians 5:17-19
Luke 12:48
Galatians 6:1
John 12:32

HIGHLIGHTING YOUR IMAGE—KEY QUOTES

Will we allow the Word to become *incarnate* or *institutionalized* in our lives?

Your greatest identity should be with being a son of God.

Identification is more than human sympathy; it is compassion interaction.

Passionate people are contagious.

SHARING YOUR IMAGE—
SUGGESTIONS FOR GROUP DISCUSSION

1. Discuss some of the areas in God's Word that are seldom addressed because we are afraid of the resulting implications.

2. Share with one another your real passions in life.

LESSON TWELVE
TRANSFORMING THE MISINFORMED

Do you know who you really are? Do you understand the purpose for which you were born? It seems far easier for most of us to imitate the life of another than it is to live our own. When we find ourselves living under the shadow of a dominant personality, such as a father, mother, husband, teacher or pastor, many of us have the tendency to assume the identity of that personality rather than processing through the journey to discover whom God created us to be. We are far better at *imitating* than we are at simply *being*.

Lest you misunderstand, let me say that I do believe in spiritual mentoring. As the father of three sons and the spiritual overseer of an international network of churches (CitiNet International), I am privileged to serve as a spiritual coach to a number of strong young men. I believe that Paul set the pattern for spiritual mentoring when he said, "Follow my example, as I follow the example of Christ" (1 Corinthians 11:1, NIV). There is a fine line between impressing those I oversee with the image of God versus impressing them with my own personality.

Spiritual control is one full step beyond true biblical authority. So many times, we see domination and control in ministry because of unresolved insecurity in the life of the one leading. When a mentor has unresolved expectations within his or her life, that person stands in danger of projecting himself on the life of the one being mentored.

As the model Father, The Image Maker has only our best interest at heart. He is not living in disappointment while waiting on someone to assume His unfulfilled goals. He wants what is best for us even when His work isn't accomplished as quickly as He would like for it to be. Walking with integrity is more important than running with impatience! He is more concerned about our state of being than our performance.

The Image Maker specializes in restructuring the distorted images we see around us in society. Wise beyond comprehension, He is infinitely patient when it comes to the spiritual, emotional and physical development of the image bearer. He is not restricted to one single method of restoration and will use any means within His infinite grasp to rebuild the broken ruins of our lives. No vessel is marred so greatly that the Master Potter cannot repair and restore it back to useful service.

TRANSFORMING THE MISINFORMED

I want us to examine the lives of several prominent biblical characters as they made the journey from misinformation to transformation. As we do, let's honestly examine their strengths and weaknesses.

Moses

Given up for adoption and raised in an environment foreign to his essential identity, Moses struggled to understand his purpose in life. Consider the emotional entanglement that Moses must have experienced. Pharaoh's daughter not only spared his life when she found him, but she also raised him in the house of the king where Moses enjoyed the privilege of honor and wealth. Acts 7:22 says, "Moses was learned in all the wisdom of the Egyptians, and was mighty in words and deeds." His life was intertwined with Egyptian culture.

But at forty years of age, something deep in the recesses of his soul began crying out for more. Maybe it was a faint impression from his childhood that he could not shake. Perhaps it was a memory of his mother guiding him down the path toward the one true and living God. Moses began to ask the question, "How does my past relate to my future?" To ignore the past is to stagnate the present.

After four decades of absence, Moses made his first pilgrimage back to the tents of Israel. And somewhere between the luxury of Egypt and the squalor of Israel, he crossed a line from which he could not return. Hebrews 11:24-26 says:

> By faith Moses, when he was come to years, refused to be
> called the son of Pharaoh's daughter; choosing rather to
> suffer affliction with the people of God, than to enjoy the
> pleasure of sin for a season; esteeming the reproach of
> Christ greater riches than the treasures in Egypt: for he
> had respect unto the recompense of the reward.
>
> —KJV

With half of his life completed, Moses began the search to discover who he truly was. Through a series of encounters with the
great "I AM," he began to see whom The Image Maker had created
him to be.

Abraham

When Abram received the prophetic word that he was going to be
the father of a son, he was seventy-five years old. His wife, Sarai,
was also past the age of childbearing. In fact, she had been barren
her entire life. Abram and Sarai saw themselves as an aging, childless couple with no hope for an heir. They were bound with an
image of barrenness.

That's why The Image Maker gave Abram more than a verbal
promise. God took him out under the stars, and said, "Take a look
at the heavens, *tell* the stars if you are able to number them, so shall
your seed be" (Genesis 15:5, KJV, emphasis added). What was God
doing on this prophetic field trip? He was replacing Abram's image
of barrenness with the image of abundance. He was burning a new
image of prosperity into the soul of Abram. God began to form an
image of victory in the soul of Abram.

Abram only received two confirmations during the twenty-four
year period from the promise to the product. Yet many Christians
struggle with insecurity concerning their destiny if God doesn't
reassure them on a weekly basis. I wonder if you are prepared to
walk in faith concerning the promise of your inheritance, even if
you don't receive another confirmation for twelve years?

In spite of this prolonged silence, Abram did not stagger at the
promise of God through unbelief, but was strong in faith. Even
when he took matters into his own hands with Hagar, he wasn't

struggling with God's *promise*—he was wrestling with God's *timing*.

When the image starts to grow dim, God replaces it with a greater image by changing Abram's and Sarai's names. *Abraham* is defined as "the father of many nations," and *Sarah* means "princess" or "mother of a prince." Every time this childless couple hears the name *Abraham* or *Sarah*, they are in essence hearing "Daddy" or "Mama." God is reconstructing Abraham's inner image into one of victory.

He did this by working on the vision of his self-image. God began to unlock the power of Abraham's righteous imagination. According to Romans 4:17, this is the process of calling "those things which do not exist as though they did." Let me ask you a simple question: What are imaginations? They are images! They are pictures painted on the canvas of our memories by thoughts. Thought pictures.

Your imagination is a God-ordained tool that can and should be used for the sake of righteousness in the earth. Even though power-hungry pagans have perverted this ability, your imagination is not an evil thing. Those imaginations that are wrong (even dangerous) are the ones that exalt themselves against the knowledge of God. But once you have come to the knowledge of the will of God, then you have the right to use your imagination in order for His purpose to be fulfilled in your life. In essence, you have to *see* it *before* you see it. God is looking for people who will spend enough time in His Word and in His presence to affect what they see on the inside of them.

Abraham spent his entire life looking for something he had already seen. Even when it came to the sacrifice of his son, he used the brush of faith to paint an image of the resurrection of Isaac on the canvas of his soul! He saw this young man blessing the nations. He saw his promised seed as innumerable as the stars in the heavens and the grains of sand on the seashore. He saw the final product even before the journey began.

Jacob

Born as a twin to Esau, Jacob seems to have wrestled with the inner issue of his essential identity from the beginning. He struggled with insecurity because he lacked the affirmation of his father. Genesis 25:28 reveals the tensions found present in this family when it declares, "And Isaac loved Esau because he ate of his game, but Rebekah loved Jacob." Obviously, Isaac showed favoritism toward Esau, while leaving Jacob to be loved by his mother. Very seldom is one raised in this kind of environment without experiencing the scars of rejection.

Jacob was uncomfortable with himself. He wasn't happy to be who he was. His history is filled with failure and disappointment: Overlooked by his father, manipulated by his mother, rejected by his brother, cheated by his father-in-law. He married an ugly woman while romancing a beauty. The one constant in Jacob's life was that he was not happy to be Jacob.

But God had a plan and a purpose for Jacob and He brought Jacob to a time and a place where that plan could begin to be fulfilled—a place where God could give Jacob the blessing intended for him alone. You have to be *you* to be blessed of God.

We discover Jacob sitting alone beside the brook Jabbok. "Then Jacob was left alone; and a Man wrestled with him until the breaking of day" (Genesis 32:24). Jacob was not necessarily alone by choice; he was alone by divine arrangement. "Then Jacob was *left* alone. . . ." God often uses isolation to prepare us for a visitation.

At the close of this long night, the Man with whom Jacob had wrestled said, "Your name shall no longer be called Jacob, but Israel; for you have struggled with God and with men, and have prevailed" (Genesis 32:28). In one moment of time, after a lifetime of futility, God unveiled Jacob's essential identity, and he discovered whom he was created to be.

Other Examples

The Bible gives us many other examples of God's people coming to the realization of their essential identity. When Peter realized that Jesus of Nazareth was the Son of the living God, Jesus responded by unveiling Peter's essential identity. ". . . God bless you, Simon, son of Jonah! . . . And now, I'm going to tell you who you are, *really* are. You are Peter, a rock."—Matthew 16:17-18, The Message

Saul of Tarsus (who became Paul the Apostle) had such a revolutionary identity change that he eventually said, "The old me is no longer alive; a new man has replaced him."

The story of King Cyrus is found in Ezra 1. A scribe came to Cyrus one day with the writings of the Prophets. This scribe asked the question that radically altered Cyrus's destiny, "Have you seen your name in the Book?" Although King Cyrus was following a course of natural lineage, God had something greater for him than the image of his father. The scribe showed Cyrus the words of the prophet, written two hundred years earlier, declaring, "[Cyrus] is My shepherd, and he shall perform all My pleasure" (Isaiah 44:28). When King Cyrus saw his name in the Book, he embraced his destiny and radically altered the course of human history.

IS YOUR NAME IN THE BOOK?

The beauty of the Word of God is that when we really come to terms with who we are in the family of God, we begin to see ourselves in the Book. No, our personal name cannot be found in the Scriptures, but our identity in Christ can be found. Our destiny as the new creation is clearly present. But we must have eyes to see it.

When you discover the reality of your identity in Christ, everything in your world begins the process of conforming to who you are. Have you seen your name in the Book? For those who are searching, you will find your identity in the same Book that Jesus did. Although He was fully God, He laid aside His deity when He became a man, and in His humanity, He had to study the Scriptures to discover who He was.

> The spirit of the Lord is upon Me, because He has anointed Me to preach the gospel to the poor; He has sent Me to heal the brokenhearted, to proclaim liberty to the captives and recovery of sight to the blind, to set at liberty those who are oppressed.
>
> —*Luke 4:18*

Following His baptism in the Jordan River at the hands of John the Baptist, Jesus heard a voice from heaven confirming His essential identity. When Jesus came to faith in who He was, nothing could stand in His way. Likewise, when you come to faith in who you are in Christ, nothing shall effectively withstand you.

Perhaps you have been duped into believing the misinformation that has been disseminated by the enemy in his desperate attempt to deceive you into believing that you are less than God created you to be. The time has come to shake yourself free from insignificance and insecurity once and for all. As a child of God, you occupy the highest position in the universe, just under The Image Maker Himself. You have ultimate worth and value. Believe it!

> To him who overcomes I will give some of the hidden manna to eat. And I will give him a white stone, and on the stone a new name written which no one knows except him who receives it.
>
> —*Revelation 2:17,* emphasis added

DISCOVERING YOUR IMAGE

Several principles incorporated in this lesson are listed below. In your own words, write a brief summary of each principle as you understand it. Or if you choose, you may copy one or two statements from the book.

1. It seems far easier for most of us to imitate the life of another than it is to live our own.

2. Spiritual control is one full step beyond true biblical authority.

3. The example of Moses illustrates how the culture, education and luxury of a foreign environment could not prevent the unveiling of his essential identity and purpose in life.

4. Abraham's example illustrates the power of prophetic words and visions to change our lives.

5. Jacob's story illustrates how the patience and power of God can overcome a dysfunctional family environment and resulting lack of essential identity.

6. The beauty of the Word of God is that when we really come to terms with who we are in the family of God, we begin to see ourselves in the Book.

FORMING YOUR IMAGE

The following principles are presented in a format that focuses on personal application. In the space provided after each, write what seems applicable to you.

1. Do you think that you have tried to imitate a dominant personality rather than discover and cultivate your essential identity? If so, explain who and how.

2. Are you now, or have you ever been, in a church or a group

where the leadership attempted to exert spiritual control? Explain.

3. Do you recognize educational and cultural influences in your life contrary to who you are in Christ and His purpose for your life? If so, explain how these cannot prevent you from being all that God has purposed.

4. Share any prophetic word of vision relating to your identity and purpose in life.

5. Have you (or someone you know) allowed a dysfunctional family situation to shape your life. Explain.

6. Find several Bible statements and rewrite them, inserting your name where applicable.

REINFORCING YOUR IMAGE

True/False

1. It is easier to be who we are than to imitate the life of another.
   True_____ False_____

2. God gave Abram prophetic visions. True_____ False_____

3. God is more concerned with our performance than our state of being. True_____ False_____

4. Abram only received two confirmations during the twenty-four-year period from the promise to the product.
   True_____ False_____

Multiple Choice

5. Domination and control in ministry results from
   (A) a sincere desire to help others
   (B) unresolved insecurity in the life of the leader

(C) knowing the right answers

6. Moses' example shows us that
   (A) you can't escape or overcome the effects of your early environment
   (B) God's purpose is greater than our environment
   (C) we shouldn't study anything from a foreign culture

7. Our imagination is
   (A) a God-ordained tool
   (B) foolishness
   (C) carnal

8. Jacob struggled with insecurity because
   (A) he was a twin
   (B) he lacked the affirmation of his father
   (C) his mother did not love him

Fill in the Blanks

9. God replaced Abram's image of _____ with the image of _____.

10. When Abram took matters into his own hands with Hagar, he wasn't _____ with God's _____, he was _____ with God's _____.

11. Once you come to the knowledge of the _____ of God, you have the right to use your _____ in order for His _____ to be fulfilled.

12. As a child of God, you occupy the _____ _____ in the _____, just under the _____ _____ Himself.

STRENGTHENING YOUR IMAGE—KEY BIBLE VERSES

In the space below write the key Bible verse from this lesson. You might also want to memorize them.

1 Corinthians 11:1
Hebrews 11:24-26
Acts 7:22
Romans 4:17
Genesis 15:5
Genesis 25:28
Genesis 32:28
Matthew 16:17-18
Luke 4:18
Revelation 2:17

HIGHLIGHTING YOUR IMAGE—KEY QUOTES

We are better at imitating than at simply being.

Your imagination is a God-ordained tool.

You have to be *you* to be blessed of God.

You have ultimate worth and value. Believe it!

SHARING YOUR IMAGE— SUGGESTIONS FOR GROUP DISCUSSION

1. Mention examples of spiritual control that exceeds Bible authority. Explore the motives behind these.

2. Let each member of the group tell which biblical character used in this lesson he or she most identifies with and why. (You could also use other biblical characters.)

NOTES

INTRODUCTION

1. William James, *The Principles of Psychology* (Cambridge: Harvard University Press, 1893), volume 1, chapter 10.

LESSON ONE

1. Quoted in Walter Truett Anderson, *Reality Isn't What It Used to Be: Theatrical Politics, Ready-to-Wear Religion, Global Myths, Primitive Chic, and Other wonders of the Postmodern World* (San Francisco: Harper & Row, 1990), 51.
2. Tom Stoppard quote taken from Internet search on "creation-evolution" quotes.
3. Joseph Stalin, *Works* (Moscow and London: 1952/3), vol. 1, p. 304. Cited in Wetter, *Dialectical Materialism*, 325.
4. Ibid.
5. Gene Edward Veith, Jr., *Postmodern Times* (Wheaton: Crossway Books, 1994), 75.
6. Ravi Zacharias, *Shepherding a Soul-Less Culture* (Atlanta: Just Thinking, Spring/Summer 1999), 2.
7. Jewel Kilcher, "Hands," copyright © 1998 WB Music Corp./Wiggly Tooth Music, ASCAP.

LESSON TWO

1. Quoted in Philip Yancey, *Finding God in Unexpected Places*, 115.
2. Myles Munroe, *Understanding Your Potential* (Shippensburg: Destiny Image Publishers, 1991), 23.

LESSON THREE

1. David Needham, *Birthright* (Sisters, OR: Multnomah Publishers, Inc., 1999), 30.
2. C.S. Lewis, *The Problem of Pain* (New York: Macmillian, 1948), 70-71.

LESSON FOUR

1. Needham, *Birthright*, 62.

LESSON FIVE

1. Needham, *Birthright*, 132.
2. Yancey, Brand, *Fearfully and Wonderfully Made*, 47.

LESSON SEVEN

1. Bruce Narramore, *Freedom From Guilt* (Eugene, OR: Harvest House, 1974), 90.
2. McGee, *The Search for Significance*, 55.
3. Ibid., 59.

LESSON NINE

1. E. W. Kenyon, *Two Kinds of Righteousness* (n.p.: Kenyon's Gospel Publishing Society, Inc., 1996), 9.
2. Oliver Sacks, *An Anthropologist on Mars* (New York: Vintage Books, 1995), 113-114.

LESSON TEN

1. Reid, Virkler, Langstaff, Laine, *Seduction? A Biblical Response* (New Wilmington: Son-Rise Publications, 1986), 5.
2. F.J. Huegel, *Bone of His Bone* (Grand Rapids: Zondervan, n.d.), 13.
3. Quoted in Tim Hansel, *Holy Sweat* (Dallas: Word Publishing, n.d.), 29.

LESSON ELEVEN

1. Mario Murillo, *Fresh Fire* (Danville, CA: Anthony Doulas Publishing), 15.